THE MOTOR CAR
IN ART

THE MOTOR CAR IN ART

SELECTIONS FROM THE RAYMOND E. HOLLAND AUTOMOTIVE ART COLLECTION

BY JOHN J. ZOLOMIJ

PHOTOGRAPHY BY BRADLEY A. SCHAEFFER
DESIGN BY MICHAEL PARDO

AUTOMOBILE QUARTERLY PUBLICATIONS

A **FOULIS** Motoring Book

First published 1990
© Automobile Quarterly 1990

This edition published by:
Haynes Publishing Group
Sparkford, Nr Yeovil, Somerset, BA22 7JJ.
England

Produced by Automobile Quarterly, Inc.
420 North Park Road
Wyomissing, PA 19610-2918, USA

President: Glenn F. Johns
Editor for this Book: Julie Fenster
Editorial Assistant: Vivian Einsel

Typesetting by Kutztown Publishing Company, Inc.,
Kutztown, Pennsylvania

Printing and Binding by Ringier America,
New York, New York

Color Separations by Red Rose Graphics, Ltd.
Lancaster, Pennsylvania

ISBN 0-85429-884-3

This book is dedicated to Caroline, Jessica, Stephanie, Jonathan, Annie and Pete

Simply, thank you!

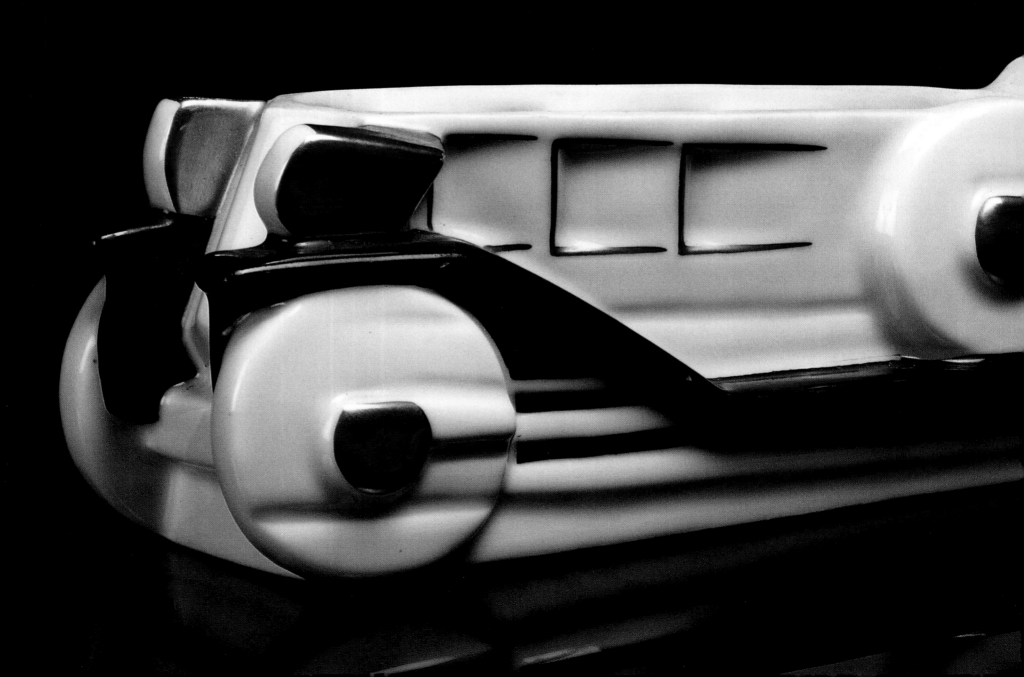

CONTENTS

AUTHOR'S INTRODUCTION

FOR COUNTLESS MILLENNIA, humans have sought new, easier methods of transportation. The human record throughout history demonstrates the progression from walking through the experimenters who conducted countless experiments with the domestication of animals. This was followed by animals powering vehicles with sledges and wheels, through "contraptions" as well as sophisticated equipment that used wind, water, wood, steam, and other energy sources in search of the self-propelled vehicle. The Industrial Revolution in Europe allowed for a myriad of land transportation technologies to emerge in Europe in the eighteen-eighties. Credit is most often attributed to the genius of Karl Benz and Gottlieb Daimler for assembling the technology of the vehicle and engine respectively. The result was the motor car. Their fame symbolizes the totality of effort made by the visionaries, thinkers, inventors, scientists and others who contributed to the arrival of the automobile into daily life at the turn of the century.

Artists, too, sought to capture realism and spiritualism in the speed, energy and motion of the automobile. Aime-Jules Dalou created the first significant monument to commemorate Emile Levassor, victor of the Paris-Bordeaux Race of June 11-13, 1895, and it still stands in the park at Porte Maillot outside of Paris. Other studios in France around the same time led the way in two-dimensional, metal and ceramic art. Soon, the impact of the automobile would be assessed and incorporated into works produced in the schools of Expressionism, Fauvism, and Cubism and Futurism. The "Age of The Automobile" would be brought to light throughout Europe and then America in two-dimensional form by both fine artist and illustrators, as well as sculptors, ceramicists, and scores of artisans at all levels of society. So popular was the art focusing on automobiling, that the Automobile Club of France sponsored the very first automotive art show in December, 1905 at its headquarters on the Place des Concorde. Sixty-eight artists representing Belgium, France, Germany, Great Britain, Italy, Spain and the United States exhibited approximately 214 works of art, some of which are found in this book.

The subject of automotive art as presented in this book is "global" in its content and origins. In researching and preparing the materials for publication, it was necessary to seek out some of the foremost authorities and institutions in the world, particularly Western Europe and the United States, to obtain information, fact, opinion and perspective of the subject. Additionally, other persons were sought to assure conformity of statements that are oftentimes modified in meaning with changes in national language and professional language. It is all those people, who assisted in such a monumental effort, that I wish to thank.

First and foremost, I extend the greatest of thanks to Ray Holland, whose commitment to automotive art inspired not only this book, but a new appreciation among those who have seen his collection in person. I am also indebted to Charles Schalebaum, internationally-known dealer of automotive art, who ferreted many

of the great objects in the Raymond E. Holland Automotive Art Collection, the art object source for this entire book; England's D.B. Tubbs, author of *Art and the Automobile*, who spent countless hours reviewing major sections of text for historical fact and structure; Count Godfrey de Beauffort of Belgium for his assistance with two-dimensional and bronze works; and Dr. William Clark of Cedar Crest College in America for reviewing outlines, art vocabulary and, in particular—ceramic origins and techniques.

Special thanks are also given to Peter Richley, who stewards the finest collection of books and articles on the automobile in Europe; David K. Bausch, owner of one of America's largest automobilia and toy collections; Joseph Freeman, owner and master international restorer from TIN TOY Works, INC.; Stanley Wanlass, America's foremost automotive artist; Dr. Riley Greene, art historian and appraiser, and John Katz, former executive editor of *Automobile Quarterly* magazine, for reviewing and commenting on the quality and structure of text materials. A special thanks is offered to Brian Schell and Michelle Van Norman for their cataloguing and research contributions.

A special appreciation is extended to Richard Teague, formerly of American Motors; Donald Meyer, automobile enthusiast and collector; Keith Fletcher, London rare book dealer and collector; Thomas Sage, international toy dealer; Simon and Minas Kachadorian of Kachadorian Gallery in London; Kenneth Ruddock, Jean-Phillipe Peugeot of *Peugeot Motor Car Company*, Paris; and the late Peter Helck for their contribution of significant information regarding individual art objects.

I also extend appreciation for information regarding motoring events and art objects provided by the staff and archives of The Ghislain Mahy Museum (Belgium): the Louvre, the Conservatoire National des Arts et Metiers, the Musée des Arts Decorative, and the Musée de l'Automobile (France); the Daimler-Benz Museum, the Deutscheland Museum, and the Villeroy and Boch Museum (Germany); the Museum of British Transport and the Montagu Motor Museum (Great Britain); the National Automobile Museum, Holland; the Museo del'Automobile Carlo Biscaretti di Ruffia (Italy); the Stockholm Toy Museum (Sweden); the Swiss Transport Museum (Switzerland), and the Smithsonian Institution, the Henry Ford Museum, the Detroit Historical Museum, the Heritage Plantation at Sandwich, the Metropolitan Museum of Art and the Philadelphia Museum of Art (United States of America).

A note of thanks to the Allentown Public Library, the Bethlehem Public Library, the New York Public Library, and the Detroit Public Library for providing valuable bibliographical resources for this book, as well as the archives of the Royal Automobile Club of England and the Automobile Club of France.

Continuous support and effort on the book were provided by the wonderful, patient and competent staff of Holiday Industries, Inc.—particularly Linda Webber, my able and trusted assistant, Karen DiPasquale, Ray Imlay, and Linda Heydt. Lastly, a heartfelt "thank you" to my family—Caroline, Jessica, Stephanie, Jonathan and Anna, who patiently watched the events of this exciting project unfold over the years.
—*John J. Zolomij*

THE EYE OF THE COLLECTOR

THE ROOTS of the automobile can be found in the Industrial Evolution, an epic era that marked the most fundamental transformation of human life in the recorded history of the world. The origins of the motor car were European, primarily the invention of German and French engineering, skill and talents. Behind these visible products, which brought a new meaning to the concept of human mobility, were centuries of thought and development that allowed for the evolution of the machine-tools used in the creation of the motor car. Without the invention of equipment such as the turret-lathe (c. 1845), the universal milling machine (1861), the automatic lathe (c. 1870), as well as new chemistry in the production of steel alloys that were hard and sharp enough to cut metals at high mechanical speeds, the motor car, and especially the mass-produced car, would have not been able to achieve the growth that was accomplished in this period.

Following the natural evolution from horse-and-carriage transportation, the automobile contributed to the change and growth of European and American society by accelerating the expansion of small and isolated towns of a still agrarian civilization into larger cities and more industrialized nations. Mass production of the motor car would alter the national use of natural resources such as coal, petroleum and iron ore as well as human resources, for it created manufacturing facilities that increased employment, expanded new markets and broadened the consumer base.

To capture the minds and money of such consumer markets, art in various forms and mediums would be necessary to promote the automobile. Initially, commercial-type artists performed the task of creating the images for advertising, while artisans prepared images for use on souvenirs and smaller objects. Later, however, illustrators and fine artists perceived the motor car as a theme to be used in work sold to manufacturers, aficionados, and others who participated in racing and touring events. Whoever the artist, the main ideal to capture in the artistic interpretation would be the aesthetic qualities of the motoring subject, highlighted through the expression of energy, speed, and movement.

The automobile, in large part through art, captured the public imagination by the late eighteen-nineties, when safety, technology and endurance demonstrated that it could be a part of daily life and need. Since then, the car and automotive art have gone through consistent and untiring changes in style, form and function. Such change has been evolutionary in nature and still occurs today, exemplified in the annual highlighting of automobile companies and their "new" product lines worldwide and the accompanying mass-media "blitzes."

It is the iconography of the automobile in the fine arts and decorative arts that is the *raison d'etre* of the Raymond E. Holland Automotive Art Collection, from which the images found in this book have been selected. Massive and dense in holdings, encyclopedic and widely varied in range, sharply-focused in thematic subject, and aesthetically rich in quality, the collection that Ray Holland has assembled warrants its reputation as the foremost "benchmark" of early automotive art in the world.

What makes a collection such as this one created by Holland so great? Is it nature, nurture, or change? Or is it all three combining with the passionate love for what is being collected? For Holland, who was raised as a child on a farm in rural North Carolina, living five miles from the nearest highway, it had to be all three. As a child, he fantasized about cars, knowing they could take him to places of new dreams and visions. Eventually, his success came and allowed him to indulge his passion in collecting period automobiles, which then turned to the love affair with automotive art and the collecting of it. After assembling thousands of early automotive artworks, he imaginatively housed the premier objects of his collection in a 24-room Victorian home in Allentown, Pennsylvania, where it is viewed and enjoyed by thousands of people annually.

The complexity of this man and his collection demonstrates a certain irony, if not the poignancy to be found in the Horatio Alger success stories of such self-made men. Holland, in his lifetime, has gone from the proverbial "rags to riches" in achieving many goals. One is the preservation of a single aspect of human life, such as automotive art, for all to enjoy. He and his collection represent the American dream of individual striving and success, the gospel of getting on and the Benjamin Franklin way to wealth. His passion for the automobile and its art is a reflection of what we all are, who we can become and what we are able to contribute. Ray Holland, in fulfilling some of his dreams in this collection, reminds us of the following lines by Robert Louis Stevenson: "That man is a success who had lived well, laughed often, and loved much; who has gained the respect of intelligent men, and the love of children; who has filled his niche, and accomplished his task; who leaves the world better than he found it . . . who never lacked appreciation for earth's beauty, or failed to express it; who looked for the best in others, and gave the best he had."

—Wendall D. Garrett,
Publisher and Editor,
Antiques

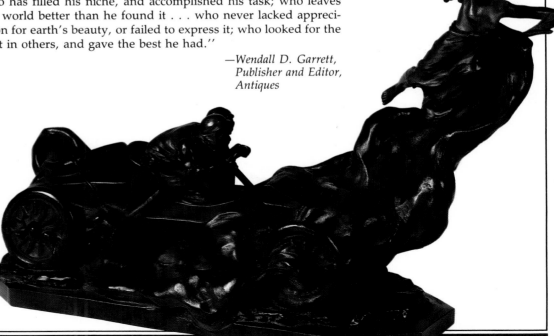

THE ART OF THE CAR

SOME PEOPLE THINK that cars first began to take an identity in 1929, when the classic era brought a new grace to both custom and mass-produced coachwork. When the car was a new invention, body engineers had nothing previous to go by; the only other self-propelled passenger vehicles were early omnibuses. It is fascinating to see the very newness in the earliest cars, the lack of precedent.

Body engineers based their automobiles on carriage technology at first; locomotives were a more obtuse influence. From that start, the development of the look of the car was a completely evolutionary process. In those days, before safety and aerodynamic efficiency became concerns, before government regulations of any sort, the look of the car responded directly to the needs of the engineers and the fancy of the customers. Focal points were established, such as distinctive grills and wheels. The car, which was so exciting just to contemplate in its first years, was becoming exciting to look at.

Not everyone, though, thought so. Farmers would throw tacks at them. They were so incensed at the disruption caused by a passing car, they called them ''red devils,'' because many early cars were painted red. It is hard to imagine the world before the automobile: a world so quiet that the hum of a car motor could terrify horses and other farm animals. This was not just an inconvenience. Many people lost their lives when the horses pulling their carriages bolted at the sight—and sound—of a motor car. Gradually, the animals became used to the automobile, and the farmers themselves were mollified after manufacturers like Brush and Ford built cars that they could afford. Even Sears got into the act, selling a knock-down car that could be sold through the mail.

No invention has ever changed our society the way that the car did. It changed the outlook, lives and aspirations of nearly every person in Europe and America. The public had an insatiable appetite for the automobile—if not the real thing, then reflections of it. Artisans and manufacturers everywhere used the automobile as a theme. It is hard to name any item that was not adorned with an automobile: a watch, a cane, a coat button, a lavalere. Taken separately, these artifacts are charming, but as a group, they demonstrate the international obsession with the automobile.

Serious artists, too, were inspired by the shape and implication of the automobile. In motion or standing still, it was a worthy, new subject.

A generation ago, interest in automobilia of this sort was rare. When I began going to antique shows in the Fifties, such items were passed up. I would buy just about anything that had a car on it, though. Today, the history of the automobile is so popular that the art and artifacts surrounding it are keenly sought-after.

The first years of the automobile were full of change, both in the cars themselves and the ways that people responded to it. I once asked my mother, who was born in 1888, if she could live in any era in history what it would be. She said that she couldn't have picked out another that she would have preferred. It was an incredible time.

—*Richard Teague*

1
PAINT & INK

ALMOST AS LONG as there have been automobiles, there have been people who longed to own one. By the early years of the century, it had become a pervasive symbol inviting associations of power, speed and independence. All that remained for automobile companies was the ongoing need to improve technology, expand production and contain costs, in order to conquer the ever broadening consumer marketplace. The question of how to take this "toy of the rich" and make it a "toy of the common man" would be answered on the grand scale through the abilities of men like Henry Ford and Herbert Austin.

As the industry grew, the quality and quantity of art surrounding the automobile grew with it. This chapter is about two-dimensional or flat art. The flat image has its own special magic, because it allows us to perceive context, space and light. Flat art has an appeal in the automotive art circle because it presents the automobile in a "world" in which certain conditions exist, or where events relating to the automobile have or are happening. The image can manifest all of these things because of the artist's talents and abilities.

In the case of the automobile, its emergence in Europe coincided with the Impressionist, Art Nouveau and Post-Impressionist periods. Of these styles, Impressionism and Art Nouveau were most influential on art reflecting this new machine of mobility.

The images portrayed were always more than a description of the artistic styles of the period. A naive and amateurish work such as "The First American Race" may have reflected the poignancy of an artist's desire to get things right on a two-dimensional surface. The trained artist, on the other hand, always had more to say in his work than merely what was presented. Observing these works always has given the viewer a privileged position, that of being above or below the plane of action. The viewer can be made to confront the approach of a speeding automobile in Harvey Dunn's "Cut at René" or left to watch another race car pass in William A. Foster's "Racers At Speed." The radiant light of the afternoon sky in Mathias J. Alten's "Towering View" establishes a different type of feeling than the glowing light found in the faces of McClelland Barclay's "Chance Encounter." Yet

"The First American Race"

Unsigned. Gouache on cardboard, 25 x 19; America, ca. 1895. The earliest known American art work with a racing theme, this piece depicts six primitive motor cars passing grandstands at speed. The image appears to be the work of a self-taught artist who may have captured such scenes for a local newspaper or magazine. Details within the piece indicate that the event took place on a dirt horse track and probably occurred on Independence Day, July 4. The driver of the foremost car bears a striking resemblance to Elwood Haynes of Kokomo, Indiana who, on July 4, 1894, ran his horseless buggy through his town. In later years, Haynes continued to participate in races on July 4; perhaps this work recorded one of those early events.

both images allow the observer to feel that he possesses the moment, because it may stimulate his mind to recapture a moment in his own memories or desires. The automobile, as a subject of art, has created its own romance, consisting of danger, adventure, power and control. The skillful artists have used it in imagery to fulfill the human ego and its need of status.

Two-dimensional images of ancient hunters running and chasing quarry, found in places such as the caves at Lescaux, France, are the antecedents of the numerous drawings, paintings and prints of lurching, speeding automobiles that were displayed at the Automobile Club of France's automotive art retrospective exhibition in 1905. Subsequent proud art owners have wanted their automobiles captured by artists whether they came from some princely stable in Europe or from the assembly line in Detroit. Such depictions demonstrate how vital and essential the automobile has been to human impulse.

Our common ties allow us to understand how enjoyable automotive images are and why they are made. The means by which an image is achieved are as important as the image and need to be commented on in regard to the objects found in this chapter.

The line between "drawing" and "painting" has never been very defined and depends largely upon the degree of finish and the extent to which areas have been filled in and defined by colors. "Prints" and the concept of a reproducible image have an ancient lineage.

By the Nineteenth century, the exploitation of "lithography" paralleled the development and acceptance of the automobile. Most examples of prints in this chapter are lithographs. Binders for pigments, means of marking a surface, and types of processes are all useful considerations in understanding the unique qualities of a flat image. Aesthetic, documentary and entertainment values of such items are influenced by the way in which the image has been realized. The richness of the paintings, drawings and prints found in this chapter reveal what the image celebrates through the artist's use of space, light, point of view, and environment, as well as the incorporation of temporal features, such as fashion and gesture, humor or seriousness, action or rest — all of which can only be obtained through illusion. The warmth, touch and insight of the artist, tempered by the demands of the publisher or advertiser, all conspire to allow us a glimpse and psyche of the early automotive age.

Untitled

Unsigned. Tempera on canvas, 40 x 34; America, ca. 1899. This piece was commissioned as an illustration by the Curtis Publishing Company.

"Foul Play"

Gaston Geliberto (1850-1932). Watercolor, 16¾ x 13¾; France, ca. 1898.

"L'Automobilist"

Henri de Toulouse-Lautrec (1864-1901). Stone lithograph, 13½ x 10; France, ca. 1898. *(above)* Lautrec shows his cousin, Dr. Gabriel Tapie de Celeyran, at the tiller wheel of an early motor car, wearing the goatskin coat and goggle mask that motorists wore before the days of heaters and windshields. Of the artist's original edition of 20 copies of "L'Automobilist," seven are accounted for worldwide.

"La Promenade en Torpedo"

Juana. Oil on canvas, 24 x 16; France, 1896. *(right)* The first known European painting of a motor car in a residential scene, this painting was the work of more than one artist. Juana, the artist who completed the home and background in the painting, was a Spanish national who studied in Paris and is believed to have exhibited at the Salon de Paris. The date "4.9.96" was scrolled on the painting by this artist and is accepted as accurate by both American and European scholars and art institutions. However, the style and palette of the vehicle, with its round steering wheel, vented bonnet and honeycomb-style radiator would suggest that the motor car is an allegorical image, added by a second artist around 1900, along with facial portraits of specific but unknown personages. The term "Torpedo" in the title dates from around 1907 and is inappropriate for this type of automotive body design.

"Voiture Mecanique"

Paul Régard. Oil on canvas, 39½ x 59; France, 1897. *(opposite)* This advertising painting was created for H. Tenting, 46 Rue Curial, Boulogne-sur-Seine, Paris. Tenting built a factory in 1884 to produce gas engines. By 1891, the first Tenting automobile was finished, using a 4 hp, two-cylinder, horizontal engine. By 1896, the company participated in city-to-city races such as Paris-Marseille-Paris and Paris-Trouville (1897). The last vehicle constructed by the company was a 36-seat bus built in 1899. After Tenting's death, the company continued to produce gas engines.

VOITURE MÉCANIQUE

VITESSE de 0 à 20 K à l'heure

P. REGARD
174, Rue de Crimée
(PARIS)

H. TENTING

"Ing. Const."

46, RUE CURIAL, Paris

"Panhard #13"

Signed "C.L." Oil on canvas, 5³/₈ x 7⁵/₈; France, 1901. *(above)* The artist portrays Charles Jarrott in his red Panhard in the 1901 Paris-Berlin Race. Jarrott was assigned the unlucky number 13 and, in point of fact, did not place respectably. The following year, Panhard sought to squelch the superstition and painted Jarrott's car the equally "unlucky" color - green. . . Jarrott finished tenth in the race, falling three places behind his earlier misfortune.

"The Horseless Carriage"

Emler M'Connell. Oil on board, 12 x 17; America, ca. 1900. *(left)* The scene, depicting a horseless carriage passing a horse-drawn buggy and a derelict coach, philosophically represents the transition into a new age of mobility.

"Washington Street in Boston"

William Ladd Taylor (1854-1926). Watercolor on paper, 36 x 28; America, 1901. Taylor was born in Massachusetts and studied in Boston and New York. In 1884 he went to Paris to study under Lefebvre and Boulanger. He returned to the United States and during his career produced outstanding illustrations and paintings for books. These included illustrations for *Selections From Longfellow's Poems, Pioneer West*, and *Pictures From The Old Testament*. Taylor completed this piece for publication in the Curtis Publishing Company's series "The Century in New England." The scene depicts a stately lady boarding an electric town carriage on Washington Street as one looks towards Newspaper Row and Old South Church at the time. Taylor wanted to depict the changes due to progress, such as "high buildings shadowing the mansards of long ago which in turn elbows the quaint gables of an earlier time." Taylor, also inclined toward poetry and philosophy, thought that the "endless trolley cars, cosmopolitan crowds and modern methods" created a feeling where the people found in the scene almost "have an air of apology and apprehension as if conscious of outliving their time" and aware "of the fate that probably is in store for them" and their children, "before another 100 years has passed."

"Coach of Yesterday and Today"

Dom d'Uz. Watercolor, 3⅞ x 6⅞; France, 1902. *(opposite)* These three miniatures are the original images created by d'Uz for later use in the production of large lithograph prints. These are the only known original works by the artist on the subject of early transportation.

Untitled

Unknown artist. Oil on panel, 9½ x 14½; France, ca. 1903. In this painting, set during the wee hours of May 24, 1903, racing cars are making their way to Versailles for the start of the Paris-to-Madrid Race. The cars were led from Paris to Versailles by spectators carrying "Chinese hand lanterns containing candles," adding a romantic mood. Following a series of accidents, the race was halted at Bordeaux. Amazingly, the leading car, a Mors driven by F. Gabriel, averaged 65.3 mph during the run!

"Rural Destruction"

H. de Gailland. Oil on canvas, 18 x 24; France, 1903. As the motor car came into general use, there was concern amongst farmers about safety and disruption of animal husbandry. This obscure artist interpreted the perceived destruction of agricultural society in rural America at the time. In England, rail and farm interests did their best to contain the development of the car via the "Red Flag" laws, which required cars to obey a speed limit of 4 mph, and to be preceded by a person waving a red flag. Such laws were abolished in 1896 when the speed was raised to 12 mph. Such concerns were actually on-going and eventually led to better development of the industry through reduction in air pollution, higher human-safety standards and more efficient motoring technology.

T. Bianco. Watercolor on paper, 21 x 30; Italy, 1903. A rare depiction of Gordon Bennett atop the prominent racing cup bearing his name.

"Distraction"

De Witt Clinton Falls. Watercolor and ink on paper, 16 x 27; America, 1903. *(below)* Falls was a student of Walter Saterlee and specialized in military subjects and comic illustrations such as this work. He produced this original art for the William Clauson company which reproduced and distributed it.

"Brush With The Express"

Walter Granville-Smith (1870-1938). Watercolor on cardboard, 10½ x 14½; America, 1903. *(left)* This is an artist's study for an article titled "The Pleasures of Automobiling," final publication date and journal unknown. Granville-Smith was to create four works for the project, the others being "A Crash Out," "A Breakdown in the Village," and "The Red Devil." The artist asked $70 for the series, of which he estimated that his time, materials and expenses accounted for $42.50. The location of this work in final form is unknown.

George Gibbs (1870-1942).
Pastel on canvas, 33 x 22;
America, 1905. *(left)*

"The Card Game"

Louis-Antoine Manceaux (b. 1862). Oil on canvas, 19 x 14½; France, ca. 1904. *(above)* Manceaux was a student of Alexandre Cabanel, a prominent genre painter of the late 19th century in Paris, and he established himself as a member of the Society of French Artists in 1894. Manceaux produced numerous and outstanding works relating to the high style and fashionable events occurring in France at the time. This exceptional work depicts friends playing cards in the summer of 1909 on the hood of a Panhard et Levassor motor car. Manceaux is believed to have painted himself into the work, being the man leaning against the tree. The chauffeur has the task of making repairs. Note the casual demeanor of the cow exploring the vehicle, a somewhat different attitude of an animal toward a car than that seen a decade earlier.

"The Darracq Conquers Time"

Flohri. Watercolor, 12 x 19; America, 1904. *(below)* An obscure mechanic for Darracq named Demogeot had to replace Victor Hémery as driver for the landspeed record attempt at Ormond Beach in Florida 1904, due to Hémery's disregard for the racing officials at the site. Demogeot drove the 200bhp V-8 Darracq, covering two miles in 58⁴/₅ seconds, and becoming the first human to achieve that distance in under one minute. Demogeot was crowned "Speed King of the World." Flohri delightfully depicts Father Time passing the "sands of time" to Demogeot.

"The Puncture"

Artist unknown. Tempera on paper, 13½ x 21½; France, 1903. *(left)* Peaceful peasants arrive with makeshift uniforms and weapons to protect themselves against the chugging object with a shaggy, wild animal that has just invaded their community. The unaware motorist repairing the tire may not know that they have never seen a motor car before. However, judging by the elderly gentleman behind him, he may soon get their point.

"Le William"

Unsigned. Oil on canvas, 35 x
49; France, 1906.

"Ride to The Beach"

Leonetto Cappiello (1875-1942). Pastel on paper, 19 x 15; France, ca. 1905. Cappiello, the prominent poster artist, masterfully creates an atmosphere of motion through the foreground dust and windblown trees in the background.

"Night Breakdown"

Unsigned. Oil on canvas, 18 x 22; America, ca. 1906. *(above)* This superb rendition shows the stillness and loneliness of a breakdown, as a woman holds a lighted running lamp to aid her companion in fixing the motor car's tire. This painting has been compared to works by Edward Hopper, a master in the use of shadowing, who introduced lighted lamps in many of his paintings. This work demonstrates such mastery with the lamps brightening the otherwise totally darkened environment.

"Country Tour"

C.B. Darst. Oil on canvas, 26 x 34; ca. 1906

Untitled

Jean Veber (1864–1928). Watercolor, 2½ x 6; France, ca. 1906. *(below)*

"The Dead Cat"

May Wilson Preston (1873–1949). Watercolor, 7¼ x 18; America, 1906. *(above)* Preston was a member of the Society of Illustrators who studied in Paris at the Whistler School. In this Italian piazza scene, officers push a Panhard which has just run over the family cat, as authorities try to settle the matter with the vehicle's owner.

"Villa Poncelot-Boitsfort"

Jean Cleemput. Oil on canvas, 51½ x 39½; Belgium, 1907. The artist was commissioned by the Poncelot family to paint their newly built villa near Boisfort. The incorporation of the chauffeured automobile establishes the importance of the automobile as a luxury object of the affluent at the time.

J.C. LEYENDECKER

"Kuppenheimer Good Clothes"

J. C. Leyendecker. Oil on canvas, 27 x 19¾; America, 1926. *(above)*

"Mercedes at Madison Square Garden"

Joseph C. Leyendecker. Oil on canvas, 16 x 16; America, 1905. *(opposite)* A magnificent interpretation of this prominent car at this prominent place by one of America's finest illustrators. Leyendecker's painting was used for the cover of a special Automotive Section of *Collier's Magazine* in 1905. The Mercedes was heavily promoted on the French Riviera from 1901 onwards. After it won the 1903 Gordon Bennett Race, it became the preferred motor car of sophisticated Continental, American and British motorists, as well as the German Emperor Kaiser Wilhelm II.

"The Lady and Her Motorcar"

J.C. Leyendecker (1874-1951). Oil on canvas, 40 x 30; America, 1906. Leyendecker was born in Montabaur, Germany and emigrated to the United States with his parents when he was eight years old. At 16, he was employed by a Chicago engraving house, thanks to a large painting he made on his mother's old kitchen oilcloth to show to the company's art director. In the evenings, he studied at the Chicago Art Institute, saving enough money to attend the Julian Academy in Paris, five years later. Returning a thoroughly trained artist with immense flexibility and creativity, Leyendecker produced his first *Saturday Evening Post* cover in 1899. For the next 40 years, he was to produce more than 300 covers, the New Year's Baby series being the most memorable. He also engaged in advertising that allowed his clients to become famous, including the popular Arrow Collar man. Leyendecker's illustrations in the field of fashion set the standard for the time, as well. In 1906, using brilliant illustrative technique and coloration, he created this work of art, which appeared on the lead page of a special Automobile Section in the October 26 issue of the *Saturday Evening Post*. The Peerless motor car, the fashionable garb and the elegant lady were all part of affluent motoring circles of the time. Leyendecker painted a series of elegant women for Peerless and other motor manufacturers.

"Lady Motorist"

Warren B. Davis. Oil on canvas, 27 x 12; America, 1908. Davis was well-known for portraiture immediately after the turn of the century. In this work, he depicts the subject in the fashionable but impractical hat, scarf, and veil that were characteristic garments worn by women before the windshield came into general use. Note the right-hand-drive feature of the car. Davis won the coveted Inness Award in 1905 and was to achieve other significant honors throughout his career. This work was produced and copyrighted in 1908.

"Speed Pass"

Attributed to Phillipe Franz Norman. Oil on canvas, 27 x 28; England, 1908. *(above)* This French artist exhibited in London as early as 1876. He became an itinerant artist and travelled throughout England, depicting a variety of scenes of urban and rural life. His works, which are considered to be of the "Symbolist" school, were exhibited at two important English museums after 1909, the Royal Academy and the New Gallery.

"Horse Crossing"

Carl Hawkins. Oil on canvas, 36 x 26; America, 1908. Hawkins created this bold and spirited work in Wilmington, Delaware, as an advertising commission for Oldsmobile. American motor car companies and magazines such as *The Saturday Evening Post* and *Collier's* used large oil paintings for their illustrations, thereby providing a substantial income for serious artists. D.B. Tubbs commented that a friend of his who painted for *The Saturday Evening Post* in the earlier days of motoring had a contract that "called for minimum of 12 oil painting illustrations a year at $1000 each" and that he was allowed to submit as many as he cared to produce.

"Grandma's First Ride"

John Newton Howitt (1885-1958). Oil on canvas, 26 x 36; America, ca. 1909. Howitt was born in White Plains, New York. He was a pupil of the Art Students' League of New York and a member of the Society of Illustrators and the League of New York Artists shortly after World War One. Howitt depicts the thrill and excitement as an elderly woman experiences her first ride in an automobile.

"Flight Time"

H.C. Ireland. Watercolor, 14½ x 19½; America, ca. 1909. (below)

"Engagement"

W.G. Ratterman. Oil on canvas, 28 x 34; America, 1909. This painting was drawn as an illustration for a magazine short story with a southern American theme.

"Back Aways"

**Attributed to Charlotte Brown.
Oil on canvas, 15 x 22; America,
ca. 1909.**

"Ferry Crossing"

William Henry Dethlef Koerner (1878-1938). Oil on canvas, 36 x 24; America, 1910. Koerner was born in Iowa and by the age of 15 was employed by the Chicago *Tribune*. Realizing that he needed additional study, he moved to Wilmington, Delaware, to study under Howard Pyle, and became acquainted with other students, such as N.C. Wyeth, Harvey Dunn and Stanley Arthurs. Koerner pursued illustration and spent most of his career with the *Saturday Evening Post*, where this work was used. The spirited and technically explicit scene depicts a ferry master winching a Simplex and its passengers across the river.

"Country Furor"

H. Fisk. Oil on canvas, 28½ x 20½; America, 1910.

"Autumn Drive In The Country"

Guy Lipscombe (b. 1883). Oil on board, 13 x 13; England, ca. 1910. This prominent motoring artist was also the art editor of *The Motor*, a British automobile weekly founded in 1903. Lipscombe was a well-known illustrator of foxhunting and motoring scenes and, as this image shows, a master of oil painting techniques, enhancing the traditional landscape with a somewhat Impressionist background of color. Such color is presented in this work, which depicts the beauty and exhilaration that a family enjoys as they drive along a country lane on a fall day. Lipscombe was also a war artist for the British and many of his tank and armored-car paintings are in the Imperial War Museum in London.

F. GORDON CROSBY

"The French Grand Prix at Lyon"

F. Gordon Crosby. Oil on canvas, 24 x 36; England, 1914. (opposite) Crosby depicts Jean Chassagne in his Sunbeam leading Jules Goux in a Peugeot during Lap Three of the Circuit de Lyon in 1914. The composition of this painting was derived from a photograph taken during the race. Crosby shows the looseness of the untarred macadam surface and how Chassagne is "broadsiding" in a powerslide reminiscent of dirt track racing techniques. The artist cleverly depicts the driver's head against a white cloud, while the mechanic is busy watching the dashboard instruments or pumping pressure into the fuel tank. Overall, the painting exudes tension, commitment, energy and motion.

"At Speed"

F. Gordon Crosby. Gouache on paper, 12 x 12; England, 1911. Two racing machines pass at speed. This work was probably painted at one of the Coupe de l'Atlas voiturette races and was later used as a cover for a race day program. The sense of excitement is heightened by the perspective as the viewer feels the cars are heading straight for him . . . at speed.

"The Isle of Man"

Frederick Gordon Crosby (1885-1942). Oil on canvas, 28 x 42; England, ca. 1914. Crosby was a prominent English artist, writer and sculptor who emerged as a major influence in automotive art before and after World War One. Crosby was a staff artist for *The Autocar* and also did free lance work for private clients. In this painting, Crosby captures K. Lee Guinness racing his Sunbeam in the 600-mile Tourist Trophy Race held on the Isle of Man in 1914. A second version of this painting, with telegraph poles to the right of the racing cars, exists in a private collection in Europe.

"Sunday Afternoon Drive"

Gayle Porter Hoskins. (1887-1962) Oil on canvas, 31 x 22; America, 1913. *(left)* Miss Hoskins created this illustration for use in *Lady Laughter*, a novel by R. H. Barbour. The book was published in America and England by J.B. Lippincott Co. In this scene in the plot, the woman is covering her ear in reaction to the driver of the "large gray touring car shrieking his electric horns."

"The Stevens-Duryea Limousine"

William Harnden Foster. Oil on canvas, 33 x 23; America, 1913. Original artwork used to advertise limousines of the Stevens-Duryea Motor Car Company of Chicopee Falls, Massachusetts.

"Auto Polo"

O. Reynolds. Oil on canvas, 24 x 36; America, 1913. In 1902, a motoring enthusiast in Boston founded a dangerous and wonderfully exciting game: auto polo. Originally, the "motor polo" car driver and player were the same person, but control and skill were soon found to be beyond the capabilities of one individual. Around 1904 a second participant was allowed in the car. Numerous competitive teams were formed along America's East Coast, but injury and disability to players resulted in states outlawing the game by 1924.

"Mobiloil"

N. Beraud. Oil on canvas, 15 x 22; France, 1912. This vivid painting depicts the Coupe de L'Auto race for three-litre cars at Dieppe in 1912. The race ran concurrently with the A.C.F. Grand Prix and Mobiloil was a major sponsor. The car in the painting, No. 55, was a Scottish-built Arrol-Johnston, driven by Crossman, who retired after 18 laps of the 48-mile circuit. Scotland was not allotted an official racing color, so Arrol-Johnston "painted their cars all over in the blue and green Gordon Tartan." The artist was a relative of Jean Beraud, who directed the prominent Beraud Studio in Paris until the late Twenties.

"High Country"

Franklin Booth (1874-1943). Watercolor on paper, 9 x 14; America, 1915. Booth was a prominent illustrator whose pen-and-ink drawings were made into wood and steel engravings for reproduction purposes. Booth produced numerous works to accompany poetry and magazine articles, some of the finest being presented in a privately published book in 1925. This illustration is original artwork for a touring car manufactured by the Abbott-Detroit Motor Car Company in Michigan.

"The Driver"

Jules-Abel Faire (1867-1945).
Pastel on paper, 18 x 22; France,
ca. 1914. Faire produced
illustration work for Samson
Tire as early as 1903. Close
examination of the door in this
painting shows the letters
". . .AMSON."

''Towering View''

Mathias J. Alten (1871-1938). Oil on panel, 20 x 26; America, 1915. Alten was born in Germany and studied in Paris under the guidance of Benjamin Constant and James McNeil Whistler. After emigrating to the United States, he settled in Michigan and developed a highly respectable reputation as a regional artist. Depicted in this work is the Austin family, makers of the American car which bears their name. In the front seat are Mr. and Mrs. Walter Austin with an unidentified person. In the rear are Mr. and Mrs. James Austin and Walter Austin, Jr.

Howard G. Davis

HARVEY DUNN, N.A.
1884 —— 1952

McCLELLAND BARCLAY

"Ford Departure"

Attributed to McClelland Barclay. Gouache on board, 23 x 23; America, ca. 1930. This painting was created as an advertising piece for General Tire: note the prominence and detail of the tires. Interesting, too, are the richness of the car, and the smartness of the women—and the likeness of the man to Howard Hughes.

"Grand Prix"

Georges Hamel a.k.a. Geo. Ham (1900-1972). Watercolor, 22½ x 16¾; France, 1938. This watercolor was completed by Ham as the poster for the 1938 French Grand Prix. The design of the car is of contemporary single-seat type and was suggested by the lap-record holder and British driver, Mrs. Gwenda Stewart. The artist based his work on the Derby-Miller. Although not a Grand Prix car, it was well known for holding the lap record for the steeply banked track at Linas-Montlhery near Paris.

"Studebaker Limousine"

Franklin Booth. Oil on canvas, 26 x 23; America, 1926. Booth was a master in the use of light to dramatize automotive portraits and created magnificently detailed work. He produced advertising illustrations for Studebaker, Willys-Overland, Apperson and other motoring companies throughout the Twenties, oftentimes placing the car in grand settings, such at the Plaza Hotel in New York.

"Just Married"

P.M. Swisher. Oil on canvas, 28 x 24; America, ca. 1926. *(right)*

"The Finest Drive Ever"

S.C.H. Davis. Oil on canvas, 21 x 16 ; England, 1932. *(above)* Davis was the sports editor of *The Autocar* and a successful race-car driver. He was a keen "Sunday painter" and depicts in this work Fernand Gabriel in his Mors during the "Paris-to-Madrid" race in 1903. Gabriel started 168th in the race, covered 342 miles and finished at a speed of 65.3 mph.

"World Traveler"

Omta. Oil on canvas, 20 x 16; Portugal, ca. 1927. *(above)*

"The Motoring Lady"

Harry C. Edwards (1868-1922). Gouache on board, 42 x 16; America, 1902. Born in Philadelphia, Edwards studied at Adelphi College under J.B. Whittaker and at the Art Students' League under Mowbray. His illustrations were used mainly for advertising, this one believed to be for the Adison-style, full-length, summer-touring duster coat.

"Street Racers"

F.W. Read. Gouache on paper, 20 x 26; America, ca. 1902. The artist vividly satirizes what occasionally happened when people with automobiles met even in a crowded, congested cosmopolitan environment.

"Changing Times"

Henry B. Eddy (1872-1935).
Gouache on paper, 23 x 18½;
America, 1903. This work is the
original art for the first color
issue of *Motor* magazine, Vol.
1, No. 4, January, 1904. Eddy
hailed from Mamaroneck, New
York and worked for the Star
Company during this period.
He establishes the feeling of
urgency and power by showing
the angular view of the car as it
"bleeds out" from the lower
left margin. "Change" is
expressed with the contrasting
images of the motor car in the
foreground and the horsedrawn
carriage. In the Twenties, Eddy
produced other automotive
illustrations while working for
the *Sunday American*.

mechanics who perished during the 1903 Paris-to-Madrid "Race to Death." These two works are believed to be part of a series of at least four, focusing on men and vehicles destroyed during the race. On the left, in car number 63, are Marcel Renault and his mechanic, Franz Szisz. Renault died in the race, while Szisz went on to win major European races and establish his name as one of history's greatest drivers. Car number 5 was driven by the English amateur Loraine Barrow and mechanic Pierre Rodez. Barrow hit a dog at 80 mph, lost control of the car and struck a tree. Rodez was killed instantly, and Barrow, who was thrown 80 feet, died shortly thereafter of internal injuries. Eliott also produced other works depicting the early motoring age.

"Cars of Death"

Harry Eliott. Gouache on paper, 7½ x 11; England, 1903. Eliott commemorates the drivers and

"Bountiful"

Fielyeh. Gouache on paper, 13½ x 20; America, ca. 1905. The motor car allowed urban America to reach out into the country and agricultural America to move its products to the city more rapidly. In this work, a ride to the farm provided fresh food for the household and entertainment for the day. The low build of the car suggests an American underslung.

"Escaping Death's Grasp"

Allen Beechel. Gouache on paper, 15 x 21; England, 1904. Illustrating another episode in the Paris-to-Madrid Race of 1903, this scene captures a DeDietrich flipping near the village of Bonneval. Driven by Delaney with Grant as the mechanic, the car ran too close to the side of the road as it approached a corner, struck loose gravel, and broke its left front wheel and axle as it flipped. Delaney and Grant were thought dead, since the car landed on them, but both men crawled from under the car to the astonishment of the spectators, and then *photographed* the ruined machine.

RENÉ VINCENT

"Delahaye"

René Vincent. Lithograph, 6 x
8⅜; France, 1912.

"Chenard et Walcker Tricolore"

René Vincent (1879-1936). Gouache and pencil on paper, 31 x 23; France, 1930. In the spirit of patriotism, Vincent presents the new Chenard et Walcker motor car in this original artwork for the 1930 model. The same poster is found on the front cover of Tubb's book, *Art and The Automobile*.

"Creme Simon"

René Vincent. Ink and gouache on paper, 7 x 8; France, 1908. *(above)* To advertise products, delivery vehicles shaped like flasks, bottles and tubes were very popular in Europe. Creme Simon was, and still is, a beauty preparation made in France. This preliminary work depicts the vehicle as the product. Vincent's handwritten comments on the bottom of the work note changes needed to improve the text, composition and technique.

"Victory at Dieppe"

Henri Edmond Rudaux (d. 1927). Gouache and crayon on paper, 37 x 25; France, 1908. Rudaux studied under his father, Edmund Adolphe Rudaux, and Jules Lefebvre at the Society of French Artists. He exhibited his works throughout Paris in numerous one-man and group shows, receiving his first major award in 1907. This painting was presented as a gift to a Me. Kaulla, a lawyer friend of the artist. Rudaux captures Lautenschlager winning the 1908 French Grand Prix in his Mercedes. Lautenschlager also won the 1914 French Grand Prix for Mercedes, the last French race before World War One. The vehicle is passing the specially built and decorated grandstands at Lafourche, the acute-angle corner found on the racing circuit outside of Dieppe and facing the English Channel. The work also is highlighted by a remarque of Lautenschlager at the wheel of the car in the lower right hand corner.

"Meeting of the Monsters"

Walter Appleton Clark (1876-1906). Gouache on board, 24 x 16; America, 1906. Clark captures the power and excitement of early motor car racing in this interpretation of the Vanderbilt Elimination Race of September 22, 1906, which preceded the Vanderbilt Cup Race of October, 1906. The painting features the Pope-Toledo car driven by Herbert Lytle. Rated at 120 hp, the car boasted the largest four-cylinder engine in the race and was expected to reach 100 mph. Clark, a premier illustrator in America by 1900, was one of the youngest artists at *Collier's Magazine*. He died on December 27, 1906, at the age of 30. Clark's work inspired later masters of automotive art, such as Peter Helck, and today provides a wellspring for contemporary artists such as Stanley Wanlass and Thomas Hale. This painting first appeared as the cover page of a special automotive section in *Collier's*.

"Bugatti"

Roger Soubie. Gouache on paper, 32 x 26; France, ca. 1925. Soubie was one of the prominent artists who created original art for use in brochures, advertising, posters, and racing memorabilia for the Bugatti company in the mid-Twenties and early Thirties.

"A Moment's Comfort"

James Montgomery Flagg (1877-1960). Ink wash and gouache on paper, 26 x 20; America, 1927. Flagg was recognized as one of America's great illustrators at this time. He spent retreats at Palm Beach, Florida, and his friends were drawn from the highest political, social, and academic circles in the country. One of his "cronies" as he called them, was New York City's celebrated mayor, Jimmy Walker. This painting is a gift from Flagg to the Mayor, signed and inscribed "To Mayor Walker, With best wishes of James Montogomery Flagg."

PETER HELCK

"1907-1910 Twenty-four Hour Retrospective"

Peter Helck. Gouache on board, 12 x 48; America, 1973. *(below)* Helck captures the drama of the 24-hour race in this retrospective of the four most successful racing marques of that period. From left to right are the Vanderbilt Type Renault-35 (winner at Morris Park, 1907 and Brighton, 1909); the red Simplex-50 with George Robertson at the wheel (three-time winner in 1908, 1909 and 1910); Ralph Mulford at the wheel of the Big 6 white Lozier (Loziers had three wins and five second places); and #5 is the 30-60 Stearns driven by Al Poole and Cyrus Patschke (winner of the eighth and last Brighton).

"New York to Paris-1908"

Peter Helck. Pen and ink, 12 X 41; America, 1957. Helck produced this piece at the request of his friend Scott Bailey, the founding publisher of Automobile Quarterly. Helck later expressed concern about the "absence of texture and the distant shore" in the piece.

PRINTS & DRAWINGS

"Unreasonable"

Stuart Travis. Pen and ink, 19 x 26; America, 1903. This work was used in a short story for an unknown magazine in 1904. It depicts a farmer by the name of Scruboak saying "your 'auto' scared my horse, sir;- it was goin' about 60 miles an hour." The cocky driver, Jack Powers, wishing to impress his lady friend, arrogantly responds "Well, you don't expect an 'auto' to go so fast that a horse can't see it, do you?" It was a common tiff of the day.

"Passing Generation"

Albert Robida (1848-1926). Pen and ink, 5 x 10¼; France, 1902. *(below)* Robida was an outstanding artist and writer who produced major works from about 1866 until his death. Considered a master of science fiction, he influenced peers such as Jules Verne through his creative illustrations, found in hundreds of books throughout his career. His masterpieces were two works that he wrote and illustrated, titled *Le Vingtiene Siecle* (1882) and *La Vie Electrique* (1892). The only book that the artist illustrated concerning the early automobile was *La Fin Du Cheval*, written by Pierre Giffard in 1898. Giffard founded and organized the world's first automobile competition, the Paris-to-Rouen Race of 1894. In this interpretation, Robida uses a bicycle and motor car to symbolize change.

"Driving Lesson"

H.D. Turobeyville. Pen and ink, 10½ x 14½; America, ca. 1907. *(above)*

"Confrontation"

Arthur E. Becher (1877-1939). Pencil on paper, 16 x 21; America, 1920. *(left)* Becher drew at least four illustrations for a story set in the Southwest, some of which were published in the *Pictorial Review* of May, 1920. Becher was a student of Howard Pyle.

"Benzo-Moteur"

Jules Ehéret (1836-1933). Stone lithograph, 48½ x 33½; France, 1900. Jules Cheret was the master of French posters for the period. He studied lithography in London and returned to Paris in 1866. His Rococo influence, gaiety of subject matter and use of color were three exciting and distinctive aspects of his work. Ehéret began to sketch automotive subjects as early as 1890, but was unable to align his work with a specific product in the earlier years. By 1900, when the motor car was more common on Parisian streets, Ehéret produced this advertisement for a special blend of gasoline ether in lead-stoppered cans. Such "Ehérettes" were found by the thousands at news-stands and on kiosks across the city. This work is one of the earliest and finest automotive art posters.

"The Race Home"

Stuart Travis. Hand-colored lithograph print, 15 x 21; America, ca. 1901. *(below)* For an unknown reason, the artist did not copyright this work until 1908.

"The Interrupted Hunt"

Stuart Travis. Hard-colored lithograph, 17 x 23; America, 1901. *(left)* This print was published by Max Williams Co. and printed by R.A. Welcke, both of New York.

L. LUCIEN FAURE

"Paris To Vienna, 1902"

L. Lucien Faivre. Hand-colored lithograph print, 17½ x 23½; France, 1902. The artist used caricature to capture the victorious 16hp car which bore the family name of its driver, Marcel Renault.

"Spilled Milk"

Walter Granville-Smith (1870-1938). Lithograph, 18 x 26; America, 1901. This is one of the earliest automotive works created by this artist. It was painted for a magazine illustration and shows how cars came to America before good roads did. Here, the driver and passenger in their horseless carriage ignore the plight of the farmer in his milk wagon, causing resentment as well as consternation. Smith was a pupil of Walter Satterlee.

"DeDion Bouton"

Henri Thiriet. Lithograph poster, 43⅜ x 28⅛; France, 1902. Thiriet was a reclusive personality who created several memorable cycling and motoring posters.

BARON PIERRE DE CRAWHEZ.

"The Circuit Des Ardennes"

Georges Gaudy (b. 1872). Lithograph, 19¼ x 28½; Belgium, 1902. Gaudy was one of the most important artists designing automotive posters before World War One. In this work, he depicts Baron Pierre de Crawhez at the wheel of his motor car for the first Circuit Des Ardennes. de Crawhez was an outstanding driver in many international races, as well as serving with the Royal Automobile Club of Belgium. A monument commemorating de Crawhez was erected by Pierre de Soete in Bastogne at the point where the Circuit Des Ardennes first began.

"Automobiles Germain"

Hendrick Cassiers. Lithograph, 19½ x 26½; Belgium, 1902. Cassiers was one of the more prominent landscape painters of the period. He studied in Belgium, and resided in Brussels, oftentimes traveling to Holland to do his finest work.

Cassiers, in his illustrious career, produced marine and landscape fine art, illustrated a number of books, and had outstanding shows in Brussels, London, Paris and Antwerp, his birthplace. No other works of his are known to include an automobile. The original artwork for this print was produced for Automobiles

Germain at Monceau-sur-Sambre and was used for advertising from 1902 through 1904. Benard at Leige printed the lithograph, as Cassiers was a resident of that community at the time. He rarely accepted commissions of a promotional nature. The print was disseminated by W.J. van Marken of Brussels.

''Prime du Paris-Noël''

Albert Beerts. Lithograph, 11½ x 14¾; Belgium, 1902. Beerts' artwork was used in this 1908 calendar, which defines month, date, moon phase, and daily listing of Catholic saint holidays.

"La Parisienne"

A Villaleardo (1865-1906).
Lithograph, 44 x 63; France,
1903. Printed by G. P. Ricordi
Co., Milano, Italy.

"Frightened"

André Nevil. Stone lithograph, 17½ x 30; France, 1903. *(above)* Nevil worked for Montaut and accomplished exceptional detail work in his lithographic production. In this case, he conveys the feeling in the years after 1900 that the peasantry had towards "road hogs." The work was produced by Nevil in his own studio, years after the scene, and is signed in the lower left corner.

"En Panne"

L. Lucien Faivre. Lithograph, 18 x 24; France, 1903. *(left)*

Untitled

Emile Marie Auguste Guillemin (1848-1909). Lithograph, 17 x 12; France, ca. 1903. This prophetic lithograph, with its swirling, outgoing Art Nouveau image, foretold the congested roadways and environmental hazards that would be created by the rise of the automobile. Guillemin is believed to have produced this work after watching the Paris-to-Madrid Race of 1903 from a vantage point in Bordeaux. The number of lithographs produced in the edition is unknown, but this particular one was framed at a shop in Bordeaux, signed and given by the artist to a certain Monsieur Brue.

POPULAIRES 2 places 6chx — 4 places 8chx de DION-BOUTON

IMP.ie J. BARREAU, 16, Rue Littré, PARIS.

1903

PUTEAUX (Seine)

''The Confrontation''

Georges Meunier (1869-1942). Lithograph, 42 x 62; France, 1903. Sometime after this work was produced by the artist, it was used by Ader Automobiles as an advertisement. Ader was founded by Clement Ader, a telephone engineer, in 1900. Meunier produced this work in pastel to produce its twilight setting and depicts new challenging old. His delightful poster was unable to help Ader's business, which went bankrupt in 1907.

"Killing Pace"

E. Pryson. Lithograph, 11½ x 7; America, 1903. Produced by the Continental Coloring Company of Chicago with custom-designed frames provided by the Keiser Art Studio in the same city, this object foretells the hazards of drinking behind the wheel of the motorcar.

KILLING PACE

" THE END OF THE DAY. "

"End of the Day"

Louis Edwards. Hand-colored lithograph, 8 x 10; England, 1903. This delightful work depicts nine scenes and was printed and distributed by Leggatt Brothers, Ltd. London.

Untitled

Georges Meunier. Lithograph, 17 x 12; France, 1903. *(left)*

"Cupid's Arrow"

John Edwin Jackson. Lithograph, 11 x 15; America, 1905. *(right)* Jackson was born in Tennessee and studied in New York. He worked for the Century Co., Harper's and Scribner's during his career.

Automotive Calendar

Print, 17 x 12; America, date unknown. An automotive calendar used as an advertisement by the Alfred W. Lawfer Dry Goods General Store along the Slatington Trolley Line in Slatington, Pennsylvania.

"The First Ride"

G. Avistas. Hand-colored and signed artist proof (no. 6), 15¾ x 30½; Belgium, 1905. Note the remarque of the gentleman in the lower left hand corner.

"Bloques"

Georges Meunier. Lithograph, 14 ½ x 20½; France, 1905. The work depicts a problem in the French countryside at the time. Produced by Ed. Sagot, the image was printed by Chaix — both firms of Paris.

"La Belle Au Chien"

Jules-Abel Faire, (1867-1945). Lithograph poster, 36¾ x 47¼; France, 1905. Faire created this publicity poster for the Automobile Club of France Salon in Paris. He was also known for his pastel works.

PEKO

"The Tourists"

Peko. Lithographs, 19½ x 15½; Italy, ca. 1905. This caricature artist has captured the humor and imagination found in the male and female tourist of the time. All cars are from the 1902-04 era and the artist originally presented the works at a retrospective transportation exhibition held by the A.C.F. in 1905. Each of the characters found in the images was later sculpted and molded in porcelain as tobacco humidors, ca. 1908. Recasts of the humidors were made in Germany shortly before World War Two.

Print; America, ca. 1906. A turn-of-the century advertising print of men's coats, illustrated by J.L. Loveday of Chicago.

"Chicken Thieves"

Noël Dorville. Lithograph, 14⅝ x 6⅞; France, 1905. This work, no. 69 of an edition of 80, was hand-colored and signed by the artist.

"Want to Take a Ride on Good Tires"

Unsigned. Gravure, 21 x 15; America, 1906. (above) Advertisement produced by Forbes Lithograph of Boston for the Morgan and Wright Tire Company of Chicago.

"Renault 35 Racer"

Ernest Montaut (1879-1909). Hand-colored lithograph, 15½ x 27; France, 1906. Montaut fathered the lithography school of automotive art. By 1910, his studio created thousands of lithographs capturing scenes from major automotive, aeronautical and nautical events. Other prominent lithographers of the period, such as Gamy and Andre Nevil, worked for Montaut. Montaut is best noted for his ability to accentuate speed and motion, often distorting the image of his cars, aeroplanes or boats to emphasize power and movement. He also used other ideas, such as incorporating the quick, blue swallow in the artwork, to emphasize the swiftness of the car. The scene commemorates the victory of F. Szisz in a Renault in the first French Grand Prix at Dieppe in 1906; the car is painted blue, the French national racing color.

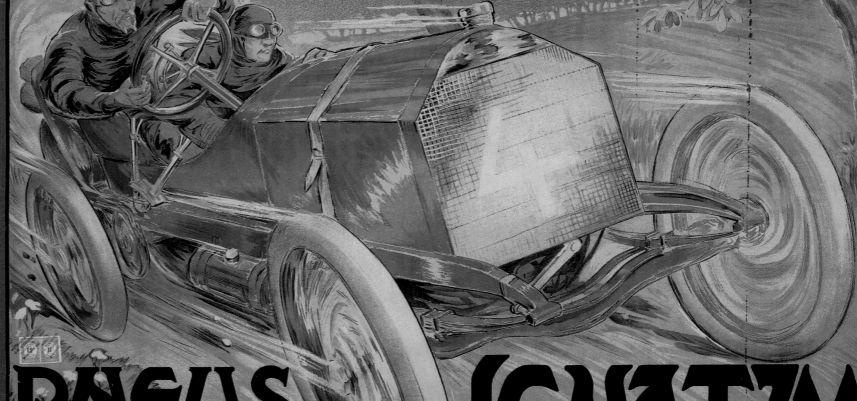

PNEUS JENATZY

10, Rue Stéphenson,
BRUXELLES.

LITH. J.E.GOOSSENS. BRUXELLES LILLE

'Pneus Jenatzy'

Georges Gaudy. Lithograph poster, 33½ x 47¾; Belgium, 1906. *(left)* In this work, Gaudy interprets Camille Jenatzy winning the 1903 Gordon Bennett Race on Jenatzy tires, but in fact, Jenatzy won on Continental Tires. Gaudy was a magazine illustrator, accomplished cyclist and race-car driver who could accurately incorporate speed and motion in his work. Gaudy was also a very philosophical man, who once suggested that ''modern speed alters one's traditional notion of time.''

''L'Accident''

Md. Assus. Hand-painted lithograph, 14 x 18; France, 1907. The artist expresses the conflict of the peasantry and the well-to-do.

"The Wedding"

Unsigned. Gravure, 22½ x 23; America, 1909. This piece was produced by Schwab and Wolf, New York.

"Dangerous Confrontation"

Unknown artist. Lithograph, 50 x 20; America, 1907. *(right)* Printed by the American Lithograph Company, this high-tension advertisement for "Republic Staggard Tread Tires" assured the viewer that a greater margin of safety could be achieved through the use of the company's product.

"Motoring Santa"

Christmas card. Lithograph cardboard, 12½ x 14; Germany, ca. 1907. *(left)* Advertisement produced by the C.P. Schmidt & Son Brewery Company for dissemination by its beer distributors, in this case being Frank P. Carr at 216 N. 13th Street in Philadelphia, Pa.

"St. Nicholas in Automobile"

Christmas card. Lithograph cardboard, 4½ x 7; Germany, 1907. *(below)*

"The Parting Gift"

R.W. Crompton. Oleograph, 28 x 40; America, 1912. *(below)* Advertisement for the Bernheim Distillery Company which produced I.W. Harper Whiskey.

"Right of Way"

Lithograph tin, 22¼ X 28½; America, 1903. Advertisement for the W.K. Gresh and Sons five-cent cigar. The piece was made by the H.D. Beech Company in Conshocton, Ohio.

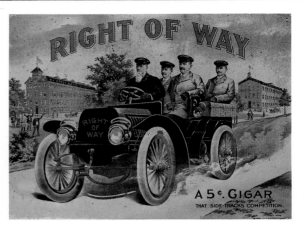

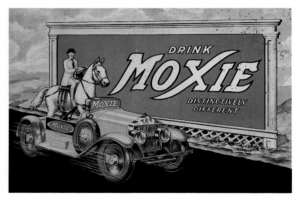

"Moxie Cola"

Unsigned. Lithograph tin, 13 x 18; America, 1923. *(above)*

"Duck Foot Tires"

Unknown artist. Lithograph print, 21 x 28; America, ca. 1910. This print was one in a series of four, commissioned and produced by the B.F. Goodrich company of Akron, Ohio to advertise their tires.

"Quick Change"

G.L. Simmons. Oleograph, 22 x 32; America, ca. 1917. *(right)* This was standard advertising art produced for the Houk Manufacturing Company of Buffalo, New York. The company produced wire-spoked detachable wheels, a viable alternative to detachable rims. Military subjects were topical during this era when the United States entered World War One. Note the anti-aircraft shell bursts around the reconnaissance aircraft and the abundance of horse cavalry transport.

"Lady at the Wheel"

G.F. Kaber. Gravure, 40 x 20; America, 1908. *(right)* This scene depicts a woman driving at speed on Ormond Beach, Florida. It was an advertising piece, painted by the American Lithograph Co. for the exclusive use of the Gordon Manufacturing company, which produced motor car steering wheels.

"Marathon Tire and Rubber Company"

Henry Hintermeister. (b. 1892) Lithograph stamped tin, 22¾ x 17¾; America, 1915. *(left)* Hintermeister was a student of Will Taylor in New York and produced numerous illustrations during the Teens and Twenties. This object was reproduced in limited editions by Kauffman and Strauss Company of New York in 1965.

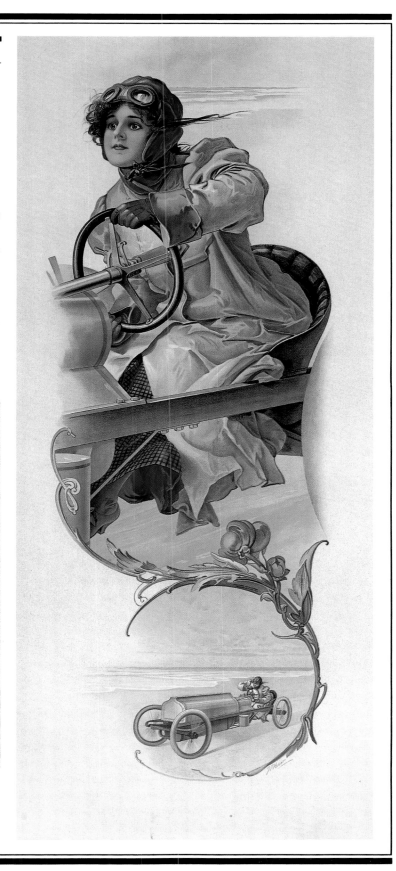

"Blatz Beer"

R. Bohaner. Oleograph, 20 x 28; America, 1913. Motorists stop from their tour in a Peerless-inspired auto to enjoy refreshment produced by the Val. Blatz Brewing Company of Milwaukee, Wisconsin.

"Riviera Departure"

Gumegaul. Lithograph, 15½ x
19¼; France, ca. 1925; no. 17 of
an edition of 250.

2

METALWORK

AUTOMOTIVE SCULPTURE, like all sculpture, describes a three-dimensional object appearing to the viewer to possess volume and mass. The medium selected by the artist for the work oftentimes reflects the period in which the work was produced. Contemporary sculptors, particularly those working after World War II, were able to create an array of works in heretofore unfamiliar mediums, such as cast plastic-resins, fiberglass and, at a more conceptional level, nonprecious materials such as plywood and cardboard. For the contemporary artist, these "new" materials were less expensive, more readily accessible and easier to manipulate than stone or bronze. For automotive art, as with all art, these materials opened up an entirely new range of innovative expression.

As this book focuses on pioneering images of the early automotive age, most of the objects presented in this chapter were created before 1930, in the artistic centers of Europe. In terms of general artistic style, all of the objects are representational, and create a sense of objective accuracy. Just about all of these objects were developed by various artists for use as gifts, commemorative items, trophies or awards.

Metal is the common medium used in all of the works presented herein: bronze with natural or chemically-created patinas; bronze with applied surfaces such as silver; bronze mixed with other metals and alloys; or soft metal alloys commonly referred to as white metal or "pot" metal.

It is no accident that bronze was most favored by European artists creating automotive sculpture pieces. These artisans considered bronze to be the most tensile and enduring of sculpting materials (as it still is), and not easily damaged or affected by movement or elements such as erosion or decay. Artists felt these attributes helped the viewer perceive the objects as a more "serious" work. Metaphorically, the artists may have sought to use bronze because it suggested a strong, unwavering future for the motor car, a mechanical piece of technology that was altering the course of human mobility. Additionally, the mechanical construct and material composition of the early motor car coincided with the use of bronze, artistically associated with weight, strength and durability.

"Madame Du Gast"

Theophile François Somme. Bronze with ivory, 9¼ x 15½; France, ca. 1903. Somme's major works were produced from 1900 through World War I. Above is a copy rendered in black marble.

Most of the artists who are represented in this chapter were academically trained or influenced in the traditional methods of using clay and wax. With these malleable materials, the artists could capture detail in the casting, with less cost for multiple castings. Foundries were readily available in Europe, many having employees whose forefathers had for centuries honed the techniques necessary in the demanding task of transforming the artist's clay or wax original into the final form. Foundries of such quality were not readily available across the Atlantic.

The work represented by artists in this chapter shares a high degree of technical mastery. Many of the artists studied under earlier masters in order to develop the experience necessary to achieve technical and aesthetic maturity. Throughout their lives, many became recognized for their work and remain historically important artists, while others were largely ignored or remained obscure even in their native land. Whatever the case, few, if any, were able to avoid the prevalent artistic changes and influences that were occurring in the world of art at the time. And none, obviously, could resist the energy and excitement generated throughout all societies by the advent of the motor car.

Many of the artists presented hereafter were obviously aware of and influenced by the work of Auguste Rodin (1840-1917). While Rodin is not known to have created any automotive works, he applied select principles of Impressionism to sculpture, particularly accidentality and immediacy. This influenced many artists who did use the car as a subject, an exemplary item being Dalou's monument to Levassor at Porte Maillot. Rodin saw his pieces in action and in light with great physical and emotional stress (particularly in his human figures). He also worked to achieve a high degree of realism in his bronzes, radically moving away from previous idealistic interpretation. This attitude and influence, not seen since the time of Michelangelo, was a useful model for the artist struggling to create an automotive object with qualities of sustained motion and action. These influences, along with other expressive qualities of the Art Nouveau Period (1880-1910)—exaggerated undulating form, line and curve—are effectively presented in many of these automotive objects. Artists depict, in many cases, the passage of the automobile through billows of mud, dust, or wind. Later works begin to stress simple, massive forms with borrowed styles from Africa, the Aztec, Chinese art and Cubism, from which emerged Art Deco influence.

"The Winged Wheel of
Victory"

Attributed to Daniel Dupuis.
Silver, 19⅞ x 10½; France, ca.
1900. Dupuis first created the
winged-wheel image in 1893
and used it on medallions
commissioned by the
Automobile Club of France in
1896.

"La Victoire-Esprit de Vitesse"

Antoine Bofill. Bronze, 12¼ x
19; France, 1900. This racing
trophy was created for the
Turin-Pinerolo-Turin Race in
April, 1900, and is attributed to
the commemoration of
Cucheret's victory in a Peugeot.
The title means "Victory-Spirit
of Speed."

"The Serpollet Cup"

S. Bauer. Bronze, 6¼ x 11¾; Austria, ca. 1902. The genius of Leon Serpollet was instrumental in the development of the steam engine car shortly after 1900. In 1901, Serpollet's vehicle completed the Paris-Berlin Race, demonstrating the endurance of the steam vehicle over the 687-mile course. At the Promenade des Anglais short-distance speed events held at Nice in 1902, Serpollet proceeded to set the fastest kilometer record (29⁴/₅ seconds). That is probably the event depicted in this piece, with Serpollet himself in the car. With new enthusiasm, Serpollet's team placed 3rd, 4th, 5th, and 6th in the Circuit de Nord Alcohol Race of 1902, an outright challenge to the superiority of gasoline engines. Four of Serpollet's cars ran in the Paris-to-Vienna race the same year, but placed lower in the results. The results for the seven cars in the Paris-to-Madrid Race of 1903 ranged from 17th through 99th. Leon Serpollet's challenge to gas-propelled racing cars came to an end in 1904 with the defeat of his team in the French Eliminating Trials for the Gordon Bennett Race.

Paperweight

Attributed to S. Bauer. Bronze, 2 x 4; ca. 1902. *(right)* This piece was fashioned after "The Serpollet Cup," and was given as a gift for participation in a race.

"The Racers"

Dominico Mastroiani. Bronze, 14½ x 32; France, 1900. *(left)* Mastroiani was an Italian artist who studied in Paris and became highly respected for his use of light and shadows. He began mainly in three-dimensional work, but shortly after the turn of the century, pursued two-dimensional works. "The Racers" was cast at the A. Hebrard-Ervani Foundry in Paris.

"60 hp Mercedes"

Gustav Gurschner. Bronze, 7 x 2½; Germany, 1904. Twelve Mercedes were entered in the Paris-to-Madrid race of 1903. The company was preparing to race a 90 hp car, but a fire at the factory destroyed its inventory. The company borrowed a customer's 60 hp car, which was driven by Belgian driver Camille Jenatzy. Even though Jenatzy did not win that race, he would drive the car to a win in the Gordon Bennett Race in Ireland later that year. Considered the first true "sports car" for the avid motorist, the 60 hp enjoyed heavy newspaper and periodical coverage, all of which led to the development of a "motoring cult" centering around the Mercedes name in the following months. Subsequent racing

success for the Mercedes team allowed the movement to grow. By the end of 1904, the Daimler-Benz company built 803 Mercedes, selling most of them in Germany and France, with more than 200 going to the United States. The company's leaders, who were fond of using local talent, retained Gustav Gurschner that year to create an art form that captured the spirit and success of their product. Gurschner used Jenatzy's 60 hp model because of its then-current popularity and the company presented copies to favored customers. Gurschner's work was so well-received by the Daimler organization that he was eventually commissioned to execute numerous busts and statuary for Franz Joseph, Emperor of Austria and King of Hungary, and another prominent Mercedes customer.

"The Race of Death"

Paul Moreau-Vauthier. Bronze, 4½ x 7; France, 1903. This work commemorates the Paris-to-Madrid Race of 1903. Moreau-Vauthier, best-known for his funerary monuments, created this work in various sizes to commemorate Gabriel's win in a 60 hp "Dauphin" Mors. The artist incorporates Art Nouveau styling in its purest form by scrolling exhaust and dust in swirling clouds, depicting the intensity and movement of the car, driver and mechanic. After completing this work, Moreau-Vauthier commissioned a version of the object in porcelain, a piece which is included in the Ceramics chapter of this book.

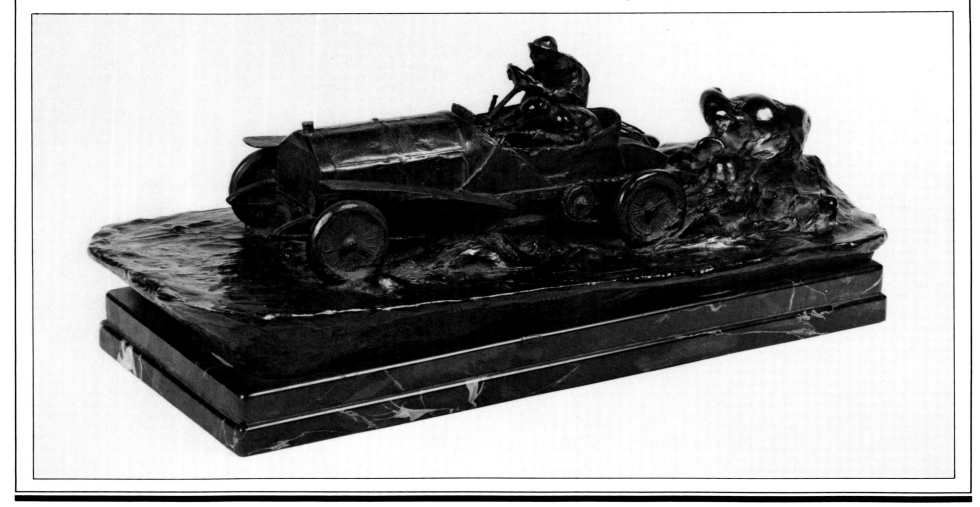

"Paris-to-Vienna: 1902"

Xavier Raphanel. Bronze, 12½ x 19½; France, 1902. This commemorative object portrays Marcel Renault winning the grueling Paris-to-Vienna race, run June 26-29, 1902, on a 615-mile course between the capital cities of France and Austria.

The first of the great capital-to-capital races was held in 1898 between Paris and Amsterdam, followed by Paris-to-Berlin in 1901, Paris-to-Vienna, and concluding with Paris-to-Madrid, which was halted in Bordeaux in 1903. Raphanel is thought to have cast six of these objects, five of which are accounted for today, worldwide.

"Motorist in Trouble"

Clement Rousseau. Bronze, 18¼ x 7½; France, ca. 1904. Motoring created its own fashions. In open motor cars, it was necessary to wear a cap, mask, goggles, and gloves, along with a leather coat, duster or "peau de bique" (goat, bear or wolf skin) jacket. Rousseau, a decorative art sculptor from Neuilly, France details the motorist's attire of the time.

Thompson Museum Trophy

C. Philipp. Bronze, 9¾ x 17; Austria, 1904. (opposite) This commemorative work depicts Baron De Caters, a Belgian aristocrat who stalled his Mercedes at the starting line of the Gordon Bennett Race of 1904. The race began next to the restored Roman fort at Saalburg in the Taunus Mountains of Germany; at the wish of the German Emperor, a Roman-style grandstand was built to accommodate the dignitaries. Jenatzy, driving one of two Mercedes in the race, was first away. Baron De Cater's Mercedes quickly stalled out. The "Baron fitted two new plugs" and came in third in spite of the bad start. Another driver, Rougier, was allowed one minute on a protest after the race, so Baron De Caters was placed fourth. Highly respected as a driver and having won the record for the flying kilometer, De Caters drove in the 1905 Gordon Bennett and other major races of the time. Contemporary motoring accounts associate this piece as a prize for races sponsored by the Thompson Museum in England during the Twenties.

''Birth of the Automobile''

Ernest-Justin Ferrand. Spelter, 21³/₈ x 9¹/₄; France, ca. 1905. (*left*)

''Chauffeuse With Bulb Horn''

Charles Ielmoni. Bronze, 9⁷/₈ x 6⁵/₈; France, ca. 1905. (*right*)

''The Peugeot Lion''

Paul-Edouard Dela Briere (1829-1912). Bronze, 8 x 14¹/₄; France, ca. 1905. Created in full stance position, the lion typifies the dominance, strength and reliability of the Peugeot Motor Car, one of the pioneers in France before the turn of the century. Its light, small-engined racing cars were especially successful between 1908 and 1914, when designer Ernest Henry and his team established the superiority of the twin-overhead camshaft engine that still dominates motor racing today.

"Premiere Promenade"
(Her First Drive)

Charles Ielmoni. Bronze, 7⅛ x
8⅜; France, ca. 1905. This
Italian-born sculptor studied in
the city of Paris and was
honored in the 1910 National
Exhibition there.

"The Racers"

M. Gunst. Bronze, 12 x 25¼; Austria, ca. 1906. The intensity and concentration of the driver and mechanic are captured in the detailed execution. The piece was probably used as a club trophy in its country of origin.

"Guardian of Speed"

Elia Ajolfi (1879-1906). Bronze, 11 x 37½; Italy, 1906. Ajolfi was an Italian sculptor best known for his statuary. This bronze is believed to be one of the objects submitted as a trophy for the 1906 Targa Florio. Ajolfi completed it and then died shortly thereafter. Lalique and Polak Aine made the plaque and cup, respectively, for the initial races.

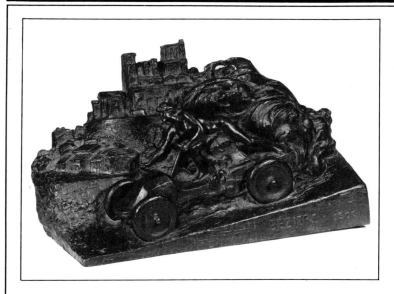

"Beziers"

Jacques Louis Robert Villeneuve. Bronze, 18½ x 29¾; France, 1906. *(left)* Commemorating a motor racing event in the southeastern French city of Beziers, the artist depicts the focal point of the city: its cathedral, atop the hilly terrain common to that region. The Goddess of Earth, Gaea, guides the Mors-styled racing car down the treacherous mountainside, amidst a swirl of dust. Villeneuve was knighted this same year, as a member of France's Legion of Honor. Other examples of his sculpture are on exhibit in the museum at Beziers.

"L'Automobile

Attributed to Ferrand. Spelter, 17 x 4; France, ca. 1907. *(right)* One of a pair, the other is nautical in theme.

"Modern Sport"

Ernest-Justin Ferrand. Spelter, 16¼ x 8⅞; France, ca. 1908.

"Mercer Runabout"

Unsigned. Mixed metals, 2¾ x 6½; America, ca. 1910.

"De Dietrich"

F. Lutinger. Brass, 5⅛ x 8⅛; France, ca. 1908. *(above)*

"Camille 'Red Devil' Jenatzy"

Rudolf Stocker. Bronze, 18¼ x 24¾; Germany, ca. 1907. Stocker received his basic education at the Institute of Fine Arts in Stuttgart, Germany. In 1902 and 1903, he completed additional studies at art academies in Berlin, Florence and Rome. He returned to establish himself in Stuttgart and was prominent in creating military busts and monuments. This lifesize bust of Jenatzy was completed near the end of the driver's racing career. Jenatzy, a Belgian, was the first person to exceed 100 km an hour in 1899, driving an aluminum, bullet-shaped electric car named "La Jamais Contente."

"The Motorists"

Heinz Muller. Bronze, 9½ x 3⅝; Germany, ca. 1912. The artist, who was noted for occupational figurines of the period, studied at the Academy of Dusseldorf and is represented in most major German museums. This artist, like the Austrian artist Hans Muller, signed his work "H. Muller." His Austrian counterpart, however, did not use a period at the end of his last name and always stamped his works with an "Austria" marking. Born approximately one year apart, and both living in the same geographical location, it is apparent that they were aware of each other's work and signatures at the time.

"Marvel"

Coffin. Nickel alloy; France, 1921. *(above)* Mascot for the Marvel Motor Car Company.

"Pneu Colonial"

LeRoy Hipp. Bronze, 30¼ x 8; France, 1913. *(above)* An advertising object prepared for the French-based Colonial Tire Company. The company competed with the top companies until the late Twenties, when it lacked the resources of larger firms to develop an international market. Hipp was well-known in France during this period for producing advertising and other decorative art in bronze and other metals.

"The Spirit of Ecstasy"

Charles Sykes. Bronze, 18¾ x 13⅝; England, 1911. Lord Montagu of Beaulieu introduced Sykes, a member of the Royal Academy and an eminent sculptor, to Claude Johnson, managing director of Rolls-Royce and described him as an artist who could design "a fitting mascot for the most distinguished car in the world." Montagu did this because Johnson was somewhat disturbed about the comic mascots which were fashionable at the time adorning the prestigious and dignified Rolls-Royce. Sykes used Eleanor Thornton, Montagu's secretary, as a model to depict a spirit who "had selected road travel as her supreme delight and had alighted on the prow of a Rolls-Royce . . . in the freshness of air and to the musical sound of her fluttering draperies." Rolls-Royce commissioned Sykes to execute the first bronze in February, 1911. Less than five weeks later, Sykes graciously sold the copyright to the firm. The company did not promote the piece until after WWI, when it won the gold medal at the Concours des Bouchos de Radiateurs in Paris. After earning this award, it was fitted as standard equipment on all Rolls-Royces. Sykes and his daughter, Jo, hand-finished each large showroom bronze for the company, as well as countless of the mascots. The early examples have distinguishable differences in detail. After Syke's death, the company continued to produce both bronzes and mascots with Syke's signature inscribed, a practice that continued until 1931. The example shown is from a series cast between the years 1922 and 1929 and was used in marketing 20 hp cars during that period. A sister to this bronze is still displayed in the Rolls-Royce showroom in London.

"Coupe de l'Atlas"

Charles Maillard. Marble and bronze, 24 x 21½; France, ca. 1914. As early as 1904, authorities of the Gordon Bennett Race discussed the possibility of holding a race in North Africa. With the advent of Grand Prix racing, the idea continued to grow, focusing on cities such as Casablanca, Algiers, Tunis and Tripoli. By 1914, the concept was on the verge of becoming reality; however, the outbreak of WWI caused the cancellation of plans and for the duration all major racing events took place in America. An unknown French racing benefactor is believed to have commissioned this piece to promote the North African race concept. Presumably, the race was to have run through the Atlas Mountain range via the cities of Tunis, Algiers, and Rabat. After WWI, much effort was concentrated on rebuilding the racing circuits in Europe, so it was not until the late Twenties that Algiers, Tunis and Tripoli began to promote races again to draw attention to North Africa as a racing venue. Not until the Thirties did the Tripoli Grand Prix and the Tunis Grand Prix reach the status of first class races.

Charles Maillard was born in 1876 in Cholet, France and was a student of Barrias and Coutan. His first major exhibition was at the Salon des Artistes Francais in 1901, where he was awarded honorable mention for his contributions. In "Coupe de l'Atlas," Maillard has produced one of the most outstanding objects in automotive art history. The execution of stonework is flawless, with the lion and lioness of the African continent roaring defiance at Progress. Bronze inlaid pieces surrounding the base depict all the forms of human transportation known on the African continent, from biped human through self-propelled, mobile human. Also depicted are men and women with their camels in caravans; scenes from the Egyptian through the Industrial ages; sail, wind and steam vessels found in a Mediterranean port, and trains, an omnibus, a bicyclist, a passenger car, a truck and a racing car. Maillard worked with the prominent Valsuani Foundry in Paris to complete these inlaid dioramas as well as the racing car attached to the marble. The car is imaginary, but highlights the Mercedes' V-styled radiator, Italian body lines and the taper-tail design used by Peugeot in 1914.

"Triumph Over Speed"

Hans Muller. Bronze, 12¾ x 12½; Austria, 1914. This trophy, like so many other smaller ones of the period, was probably produced in limited quantities as a prize to be awarded at local club meetings. The Simu Museum in Bucharest conserves the work of this artist, who studied under the prominent Viennese sculptor, Edmund Hellmer. (This artist's work should not be confused with that of Heinz Muller from Germany, also in this chapter.)

"Ballot Moteur"

Emile Edmond Peynot (1850-1932). Bronze, 16 x 10; France, 1917. *(left)* Peynot was a student of the noted French sculptor Robinet, and by the Eighteen-eighties, he began to receive national recognition for his statuary. Throughout his lifetime, he produced numerous commissions, some of which are found at Auxerre and Fountainbleau. Peynot was a Knight of the Legion of Honor and became an officer of this prestigious institution in 1903. He created this rare, ethereal-styled object for Ballot in 1917 and henceforth it became known as the "Trumpeting Lady." It was as dramatic and as finely styled as any piece of the era, in celebration of the spirit of the automobile. Cast by the artist in a smaller version *(above)* the same year for use as a hood ornament, it immediately identified the product with the company, Ballot Establissement Motor Car Company in Paris.

Italian Filigree Cars

The art of filigree has a history dating back to ancient Greece and peaked in Italy in the 17th century. Using fine wire made of silver or gold, the artisan worked metal into intricate designs to produce the form. Each object stands alone on a framework of heavier wire. For ornamentation, finer wires have been curled, twisted, braided and varied with tiny connecting beads or strips to assure support. All wires have been soldered. These objects were given as gifts, usually to the wives of motor car purchasers or sold as gifts for friends or relatives who purchased a new automobile.

Center:
Sterling silver, ca. 1912. One of the largest and rarest automotive filigrees known, this piece held pencils, cigarette holders and other paraphernalia.

Far right:
Silver, ca. 1900.

Lower right:
France, ca. 1906. Cabriolet-styled De Dion-Bouton car.

Bottom row and lower left:
These two items are examples of rear-entry tonneaus, common to motor car production from 1890 through 1904. One filigree car made of silver or gold has a semi-precious stone as its head lamp.

Hispano-Suiza showroom Emblem

Francois-Victor Bazin. Bronze, 11¾ x 15¾; France, 1919. *(right)* Founded in Barcelona, Spain, with Swiss-national Marc Birkigt as chief engineer, this Spanish/Swiss company fittingly chose the name Hispano-Suiza. The company opened a factory in Paris in 1912 and won many races with its voiturettes. During the war, Hispano-Suiza engines were used in SPAD and SESA fighter aeroplanes. France's "Escadrilles des Cigognes" elite fighter squadron flew SPADs on the Western Front, securing many victories. During the war, this unit adopted the stork as its mascot. When the war ended, the company returned to automobile production. The 1919 H6 Hispano-Suiza with its 6.5-litre overhead camshaft, six cylinder engine and power-assisted brakes was the fastest, smartest-looking and most advanced luxury car produced in Europe. The company's vision and designs continued that reputation throughout the Twenties.

Francois-Victor Bazin was a child prodigy and exhibited for the first time in 1913 at the age of 16. He was later a respected student of Navelier and Injalbert. In creating the stork for the Hispano-Suiza directors, Bazin captured the graceful movement and elegance of the creature. The mascot became symbolic of Swiss mechanical excellence blended with all that was quality in French style. It was used throughout the production years of the company. Bazin gained prominence from the work and went on to win other national prizes. He continued to have major exhibitions through the eve of WWII.

"La Vitesse"

Ouline. Bronze, 17¼ x 23; France, ca. 1920. *(right)*

"Mercury on Winged Wheel"

S. Bauer. Bronze, 11¾ x 4¼; Austria, 1918. *(left)* The object is inscribed "Tani, Christmas, 1918, My Gift, Vienna." The identity of donor and recipient is unknown, but Bauer's design emulates the Deming Touring Trophy of 1906.

Art Deco Vase

M. Paignant. Bronze, 6½ x 2½; France, ca. 1924. This piece was cast at the Colin Foundry in Paris.

Bas Relief Plaque

Huguenin. Copper, 7¼ x 10; France, ca. 1925. This plaque depicts a three-quarter view of a post-WWI racing car. Huguenin also produced automotive images for pocket watch cases during the period.

"La conquete de L'Air"

Georges Colin. Bronze, 30½ x 30½; France, ca. 1920. Originally, this bronze was commissioned by the French government to commemorate the historic aeronautical achievements of Santos-Dumont, the famous Brazilian aeroplane and airship pilot. It was constructed as a monument in Paris and depicted Icarus lifting his wings and rising above the limitations of earthly man. The Farman Company adopted the image because of its early association with aircraft manufacturing. By the Twenties, the company also used the image as the mascot for its cars. Colin was retained to produce a variety of these bronzes and also worked on the production of the mascots, which, surprisingly, were produced in England and other countries surrounding France. After the demise of the company, Finningan's of London continued to cast and sell the bronze, chrome-plated mascots for years. Colin was born at Vincennes and as a student of the Ecole des Beaux Arts, he exhibited his work for the first time in 1899. He later studied under Valton, a highly respected master of naturalism. Valton's influence can be seen in the structural and muscular detail of the Colin's work.

"Bibidum"

Unsigned. Chrome-plated; France, ca. 1928. *(above)* The mascot for Michelin Tire Company, Bibendum sets on a Michelin cable tire.

"Le Dauphin"

F. Camio. Bronze; France, ca. 1913. *(right)* This was one of 50 in the first edition, given by the London Guarantee and Accident Company, which insured fleets of automobiles in France.

"Chevrolet Quota Trophy"

Unsigned. Nickel alloy; America, 1927. *(left)* Awarded to salespeople in October, 1927, by the Chevrolet Motor Car Company. Number 11 of the edition, it depicts a goddess holding Charles Lindberg's Spirit of St. Louis.

"Race of Solitude"

Unsigned. Metal alloy, 9¾ x 24¼; Germany, 1924. *(Below)* Attributed as a representation of Otto Merz's record hill-climb at Solitude Castle near Stuttgart, Germany. The car is a Type-K, the first of the big supercharged Mercedes cars, a model that won many events from 1923 through 1927, after which the Type-S assumed racing prominence.

"Bobby"

Unsigned. Brass, 4½ x 2; England, 1922. *(right)* Foundry number on object is 689035.

"Lyon Race"

Unsigned. Nickel alloy; France, ca. 1930. *(left)* Art Deco car emerging from a cloud bank. It was made in France and it was probably given as a commemorative at a race.

Pipe Car

Bronze, 2½ x 5½; Belgium, 1904. *(above)* Given for participation in the Gordon Bennett Race of 1904.

Daimler Car

Bronze, 2¾ x 4; Austria, ca. 1902. *(below)* Produced by FBW Foundry in Bermann, Austria.

Daimler Desktop Paperweight

Bronze, 3 x 5; Austria, 1898. *(above)* Manufactured by Thenn and Kauba of Vienna, ''Geschutzt (registered) Model number 4511'' is of high quality with fine detail work. Note the radiator under the front of the car.

Paperweights

Left to right:

Bronze, 2½ x 3½; Germany, ca. 1902. This type of paperweight features recessed head and side lamps where a jeweler could place semi-precious stones.

Bronze, 4 x 3¼; Germany, ca. 1904.

Bronze, 4½ x 5¾; Germany, ca. 1902.

"Racing Driver"

Signature illegible. Bronze, 4⅝ x 11½; ca. 1927.

Mercedes Car

Bronze, 2 x 4; ca. 1905. Given for participation in Gordon Bennett Races.

Paperweight

Bronze, 2 x 5½; attributed to England, ca. 1925. *(below)*

"Renault 45"

Unsigned. Silver plate, 5³⁄₈ x
15¹⁄₂; France, ca. 1926.

"Bugatti Driver"

M. Blanc. Bronze, 4 x 4; France, ca. 1927.

"Touring Mercedes"

Unsigned. Bronze, 6¼ x 16; Germany, 1914. Used as a showroom ornament, this sculpture depicts a woman taking the air in the open four-door "torpedo" or touring car.

"Minerva - Goddess of Peace"

Pierre de Soete. Nickel alloy, 6⅞ x 3⅝; Belgium, ca. 1922. *(left)* Mascot for the Minerva Motor Car company.

"Minerva-Goddess of War"

Pierre De Soete, ca. 1928.

"Minerva Race Car"

Pierre De Soete (1886-1948). Bronze, 12½ x 35; Belgium, 1928. *(Below)* De Soete captures a Minerva racing car (number 9) at speed, rounding an uphill turn. Used by the Minerva Motor Car Company as a team trophy, several of these objects exist in private collections worldwide. Minerva cars were Belgium's most successful luxury car, using the Knight sleeve-valve engine, which was based on American patents. De Soete was Belgium's foremost motoring artist throughtout the Thirties and designed the headshaped mascot for the company, as well as full-sized statuary of Minerva, Goddess of Warfare and Wisdom.

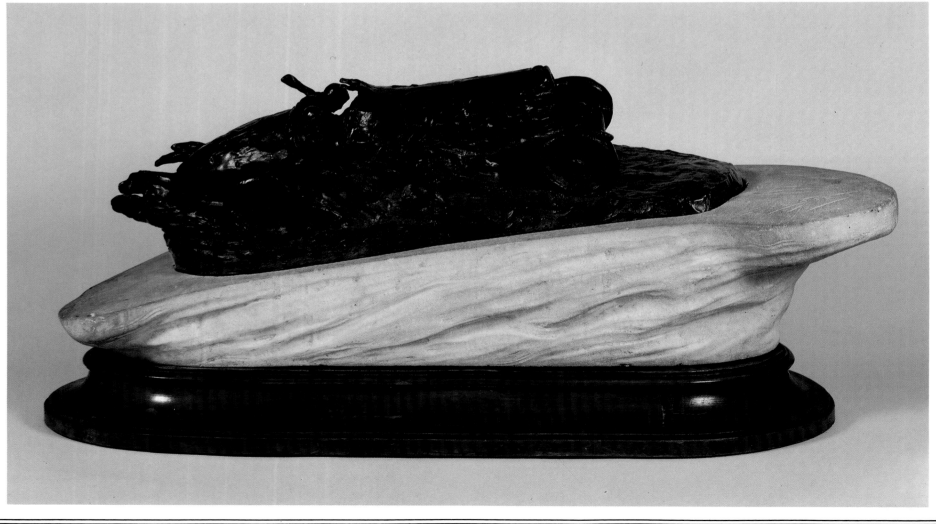

"The Race Driver"

Gustancs-Francois Pimienta.
Bronze, 16¾ x 18½; France, ca.
1925. Pimienta was honored at
the Exposition of Independent
Art Masters held in Paris in
1937 and his work is currently
represented in the Louvre and
the Museum at Grenoble. "The
Race Driver" served as the
model for radiator mascots
produced in Paris in the late
Twenties.

"The Targa Florio Bugatti"

Unsigned. Bronze, 11½ x 9¾; Italy, ca. 1928. This sculpture depicts male and female drivers passing through a laureled horseshoe archway in a Bugatti. The theme of this bronze celebrates the new roles being assumed by women in the racing world at that time. Cavagliere Vincenzo Florio actively sought female participants in his races. In 1927, Elizabeth Junek from Czechoslovakia entered and became the first female competitor in the 18th Targa-Florio. Cavagliere Florio welcomed her participation and, in a rare moment, embraced her at the starting line, wishing her a successful race. Junek was driving a 2.3 Supercharged 35B Bugatti. To the astonishment of many in the audience who were leery of the female's role in racing, Junek expertly moved into first place by the second lap. Her position changed throughout the race, but her skills were acknowledged when she aptly passed the professional driver, Divo, in Lap Four. Junek, faltering due to a faulty water pump, placed fourth in the race. Her talents allowed her to run for nearly 300 miles in the top echelon of the race and her competitiveness on that day, to this day, is considered the best road-racing performance by a woman driver in the history of the sport.

"Bolide (Racing Car)"

Gustave Miklos (1888-1967). Chromium-plated bronze, 3¼ x 10½; Hungary, 1927. Futurist sculptors like Miklos captured the power, aerodynamic design and speed of the racing car. In this work, Miklos blends organized symmetry with the natural form of the racing car. While a student of the School of Decorative Arts in Budapest, Miklos was impressed by the works of Paul Cezanne, following a visit to an exhibition of Cezanne's work at the salon d'Automne in Paris in 1907. By 1928, Miklos had achieved a highly respected reputation in Hungary and France, and was invited to present his works in a architectural sculpture exhibition in Paris. "Bolide" was one of the works presented, and was received with great popularity. Since that time, this object has been shown in various books and catalogues on Decorative Arts, erroneously titled "Locomotive in Motion," a clear misnomer when one sees the original sketches for the object, which depict four wheels, two entry doors, and so forth. Originally, Miklos cast an edition of four numbered pieces; he later produced a second casting, also low in number, but without enumeration. In 1947, he made a colorful painting of "Bolide" at speed on the salt flats at Bonneville, Utah. The artist considered "Bolide" as a tribute to men like Parry-Thomas, Segrave, Campbell, and Cobb, who advanced the conceptual designs of the automobile, allowing humankind to go beyond its dreams in the quest of land speed. Miklos' work, so deceptively simple, has always been prominent in the decorative arts and, by 1950, he was considered one of the most sophisticated artists of this field. His work has been exhibited in major museums in Paris, Budapest, Munich, Vienna, Minneapolis and other cities around the world.

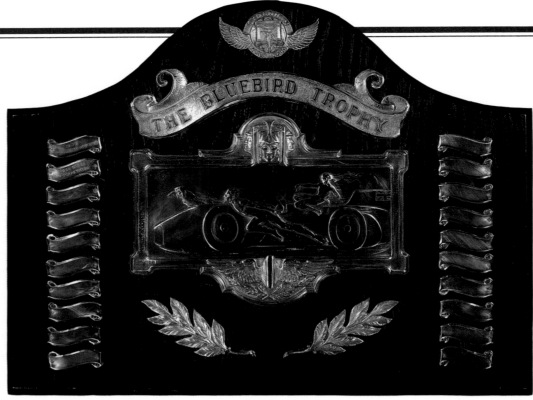

"The Bluebird Trophy"

Sterling silver, 17⅛ x 20½; England, 1933. An award offered by the Sydenham Motor Club and won in 1933 by G.P. Harvey Noble. Presumably created by a local English silversmith, the object is unsigned.

"Bluebird"

Unsigned. Sterling silver, 5 x 23; England, 1929. (Below) Commemorative for the land speed records of Sir Malcolm Campbell.

132

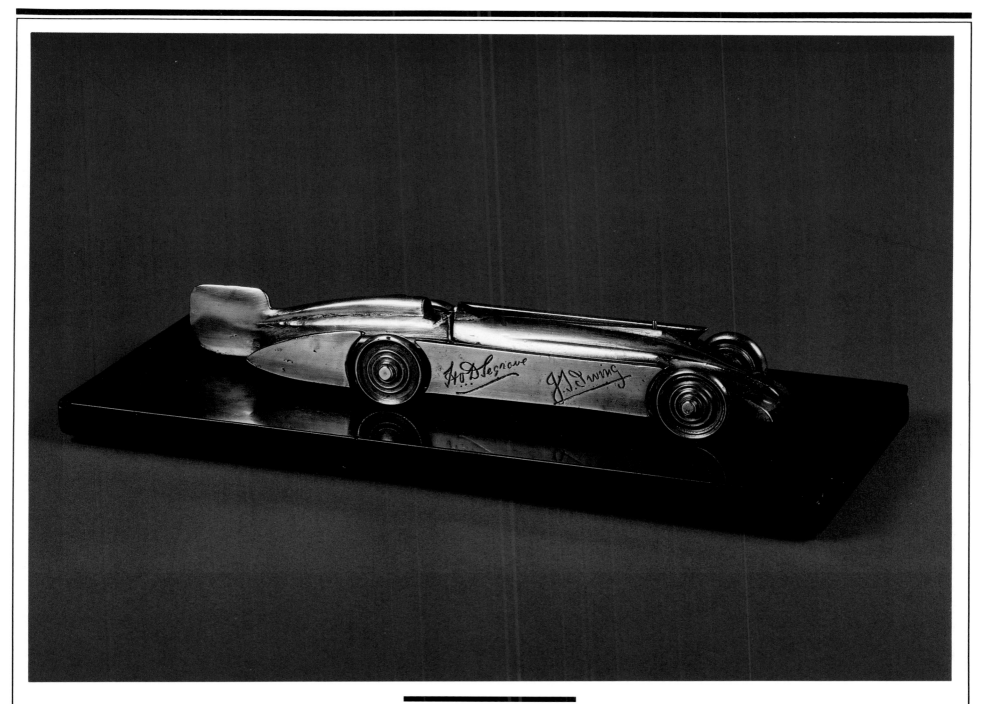

"Golden Arrow"

Unsigned. Bronze, 1¼ x 8;
England, 1929. Gift
commemorating the Segrave-
Irving relationship in
establishing the 231 mph
landspeed record on March 11,
1929. The object has the
signatures of both men
inscribed on the side of the car.

MEDALLIONS

Relief

Unsigned. Sterling silver, 5½ x 8½; England, ca. 1913. A relief inspired by an early touring car.

Motoring medallion

Frassiea. Bronze, 7⅝ x 6⅞; Italy, ca. 1907.

Motoring medallion

Fonson et Cnie. Bronze, 8⅞ d.; France, ca. 1905. The image reveals three racing cars as seen from aerial balloon.

"Sternfahrt Zum Ries Rennen"

August Rantz. Bronze, 4³⁄₈ x 3¹⁄₈; Austria, 1911. Rudolph Fuertner received this medallion for participation in this Austrian endurance race.

"Automobile Club O'est"

Breithut. Bronze, 3⁵⁄₈ d.; France, ca. 1900. The artistic side has a rare and unique winged "two-wheeled" image.

1910 International Exposition Medallion

Cristiano Rossi. Bronze, 2⅞ d.; Argentina, 1910. Rossi created this magnificent bronze medallion for the 1910 International Exposition of Land Transportation Carriers, held in Buenos Aires, Argentina. The obverse side depicts a goddess lecturing mankind before an automobile. The background incorporates a trolley in a prominent Buenos Aires street scene. The reverse side shows the goddess extending her arms forth over various modes of transportation, such as a wagon drawn by six oxen, a moving train, and a driver in a speeding race car. The object rests in a wooden and glass case.

"Goddess of Victory"

Daniel Dupuis. Bronze with silverwash, 8¾ x 13⅛; France, ca. 1893. Around 1893, the Automobile Club of France commissioned Daniel Dupuis to develop an image appropriate for its various trophies, awards and medallions. Dupuis, an artist of outstanding capabilities, created the Goddess of Victory sitting in an Art Nouveau three-wheeled vehicle, her left hand holds the steering wheel and her right bears a lit torch. Several variations of Dupuis's image have emerged on other, later automotive art objects, but Dupuis is the first known artist to have used the image of a winged-wheel in his work, which can be seen on the front of the vehicle. This particular plaque was made of bronze with silverwash and was given by the A.C.F. to Charles Jeantaud in 1901 for his contributions to motoring technology. Jeantaud led the development of the electric car in France. His greatest technical contributions in the field were from 1893 through 1904.

Medallions

These medallions range in diameter from 1½ to 5 inches. Clockwise from top center:

"Marcel Renault" Frederick Charles Vernon. Bronze; France, 1903. A commemoration of the death of Marcel Renault (1872 - 1903) in the Paris-to-Madrid Race of 1903.

"Promotion Society" Silver; France, 1904. This medallion was presented by the A.D.F.'s "Promotion Society" to P. Rigaus for involvement in the French Elimination Trials preceding the Gordon Bennett Race of 1904.

"The Spirit of Industry" Jean Bory. Bronze; ca. 1909. "The Spirit of Industry" lifts her arms welcoming the new age of technological transportation. An automobile, sailboat, powerboat, balloon, dirigible, and fixed-wing aircraft are found on the image. The frame surrounding the medallion was made by Eduoard Pelier.

"The Future" Unsigned. Silver; Germany, ca. 1908. Depicting an image created by Sir Hubert von Herkomer (1849 - 1914) in 1905, this silver medallion depicts a blinded putti wearing a ribbon inscribed "The Future" beneath her breast. Against the radiator of an automobile, she leads the vehicle into unknown and uncharted directions. The object was awarded to Victor Ludorum (driver) and F.G. Galley (mechanic) for their participation in a gymkhana (sporting event) on September 10, 1908.

"Wanderpreis" I.C. Klinkosch. Silver; Germany, 1912. Awarded to drivers and mechanics in the Alpenfahrt race of June 16-23, 1912. These races were conducted through 1914. The image presents the ongoing conflict between elements of the environment and technology.

S. Edouard Fraisse. Bronze; France, 1926. Two atlas men lift

large floral globes as they look down upon the racing driver and mechanic in this medallion. Fraisse did many medallions for sporting events and many of his works have been conserved by the Bougogne Museum. This object was awarded to a Monsieur Grabels in 1926.

"Rallye de Pentecote" Edouard-Pierre Blin. Bronze; France, 1935. Blin studied under such masters as Chaplain, Bottee and Hector Lemarie at the Ecole des Beaux Arts. This is an excellent example of Blin's combining late Art Nouveau styling with Art Deco.

Special Medallion. C. Fazerberg. Sterling silver; Sweden, 1939. A sea gull and porpoises flowing in artistic line with a driver and car highlights this appreciation medallion given to Russell E. Singer, general manager of the American Automobile

Association, the world's largest motoring organization. Gustaf Adolf, President of the Royal Automobile Club of Sweden, presented the award to Mr. Singer in Stockholm, Sweden. The image was created by C. Fazerberg in sterling silver and was completed in 1939.

TROPHIES

"Hulcan Trophy"

Hipp Moreau. Spelter, 19½ x 9½; France, 1903. *(above)*

"The Challenge Cup"

C. Klinkosch. Mixed materials, 28 x 19; Germany, 1912-14. Klinkosch was the crown jeweler for the Emperor of Austria as well as other royalty of the time. This trophy was awarded for the Austrian Alpine rallies of 1912, 1913 and 1914. The events were conducted annually, sponsored by several regional automobile clubs, and promoted speed, endurance and reliability. In this magnificent work, Klinkosch depicts the gods of Earth, Wind, and Fire looking down upon the dawning age of Technology, as represented by the Audi stock touring car designed by Ferdinand Porsche, a car that won in 1914. Audi used the image of this trophy in its marketing campaigns to promote motor car sales in 1915 and beyond. Klinkosch also designed sterling silver medallions for winning participants. This object is one of five known in existence and is highlighted by distinguishing features such as silver vermeil and enamel automobile club plaques.

"Coppa Vincenzo Florio"

"Coppa Vincenzo Florio"

Polak Aine. Sterling silver, 8 x 16; France, 1914. *(left)* This trophy was won by Felice Nazzaro, victor of the Coppa Florio Race at the Madonie Circuit in Sicily on May 31, 1914. This was the last race held in Italy before World War I.

"Coppa Vincenzo Florio"

Polak Aine. Bronze, 8 x 16; France, 1905. *(below)*

"Der Wanderpreis"

Bronze, 6½ x 12¾; Austria, ca. 1908. *(above)* This trophy was awarded to participants in the Prince Heinrich Tour of 1908 (won by Fritz Erle in a Benz); 1909 (Wilhelm Opel in an Opel); 1910 (Erle in a Benz); 1909 (Opel in an Opel), and 1910 (Ferdinand Porsche in an Austro-Daimler). The trophy represents the Mercedes driven by Prince Heinrich, the sponsor of the event. The prince was the Kaiser's brother and a very keen motoring enthusiast. The Tour, which always began at Berlin and ended in a major city such as Frankfurt or Homburg, superseded the earlier Herkomer Trophy, and it carried tremendous prestige.

"Grand Prix De La Cote D'Azur"

Louis Maubert. Bronze, 21 x 26¼; France, 1925. Maubert, like Bazin and Maillard, studied under Barrias and Peuch. He was a student at the Ecole des Beaux Arts and had a commendable, if humble, career. Maubert captures the life-like cactus, rocky coastline, and hairpin turns found along the Cote d'Azur. The car depicted is a Delage driven on the Montlhery Circuit by Robert Benoist and mechanic Albert Divo, winners of the race. The badge of the Automobile Club of Nice, which sponsored the race, can be found attached to the rock outcrop. Maubert's work is represented in the museum at Amiens.

"The Trials Championship Trophy"

F. Gordon Crosby. Bronze, 3 x 12¼; England, 1932. This object is a superb action study. Originally, Crosby was asked to cast it as a gift for S.C.H. Davis. Davis, sports editor of *The Autocar*, drove in many hill-climbing and reliability races, setting several records. He won the 24-Hour Race at LeMans in 1927 driving a Bentley. On Easter Monday, 1930, he drove his "100 mph" Invicta at Brooklands, crashing the car and hurting himself. His friends presented him with this gift several months later. In 1932, the object was again cast for the Brooklands Mountain Championship. This seems a natural way to use the work, since Crosby used an imaginary car, incorporating features from the Aston-Martin, Riley and Alvis designs along with Perrot brakes and Ackerman steering. The first bronze was cast at the Simper Foundry in London.

"Les 24 Heures du Mans"

Ernest-Charles Diosi. Bronze, 30¼ x 30⅛; France, ca. 1923. Twenty-four hour motor racing was born in the United States on trotting tracks. Peter Helck, in his book *The Great Auto Races,* credits the Brighton Beach track with the honor, for it successfully ran races for four years, the last being in 1910. After WWI, Charles Faroux, the dean of French motor sport, sought to develop the 24-hour race in Europe. Through his inspiration and leadership, and with the able support and assistance of the Auto Club de l'Ouest, the inaugural race was run in 1923 with 33 entries. Diosi was emerging as a prominent artist in Paris at the time and it is believed that Faroux, who was also a patron of the arts, arranged a commission for Diosi to complete this spectacular trophy for the race. A goddess with arms and legs extended suggests the hands of a clock and arches across a circular ring inscribed with the numbers I - XII in Roman figures and 13-24 in Arabic figures. A steep racing bank is sculpted at one side of the base. The entire image is an artistic approach in creating a 24-hour clock, clearly demonstrating Diosi's creative genius. Diosi studied under Barrias and Coutan and won major awards and recognition as an artist through the Thirties. This work, like the majority of Diosi bronzes, came from the well-known C.F.A. Foundry in Paris.

"Coupe Automobile Georges Boillot"

Francois-Victor Bazin. Bronze, 13½ x 17¾; France, 1925. Awarded for a regional event held at Boulogne-sur-Mer, this trophy honored the highly respected Boillot, who won numerous Grand Prixes and other international racing events.

"International Grand Prize"

Silver, 25 x 19; America, 1908. This race was created by the Automobile Club of America in cooperation with the Savannah Motor Club. The event covered 402 miles. Wagner earned the trophy in a Fiat.

Presentation Tray

Silver, 14³⁄₈ x 17¹⁄₈; France, 1904. *(right)* Awarded to Léon Théry, winner of the French Elimination Trials at the Circuit de L'Argonne on May 20, 1904 and the Gordon Bennett Cup at the Taunus Circuit on June 17, 1904. In both events, he drove an 80hp Richard-Brazier equipped with newly developed shock absorbers, which significantly contributed to his success.

"Vanderbilt Toasting Cups"

Silver, 4 x 2¹⁄₂; America, 1908. These miniature toasting cups are made in the likeness of the William K. Vanderbuilt, Jr. Cup, a trophy presented for competition through the American Automobile Association. These cups were given as a commemorative of George Robertson's victory in his Locomobile in the fourth Vanderbilt Cup race in 1908, which was the first time the event was won by an American. The toasting cups are classical in form and depict the image of Vanderbilt as he appeared in his 90hp Mercedes on the beach at Ormond, Florida in 1904.

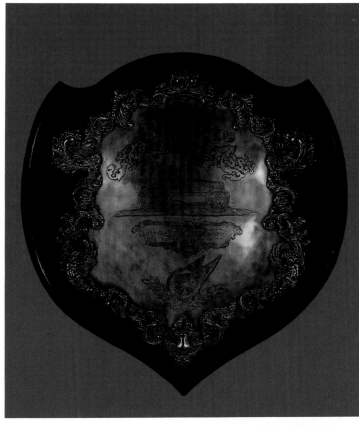

"Bay State Automobile Association"

Unsigned. Copper alloy, 16 x 14½; America, 1910. *(left)* This second prize trophy was awarded to G. Reed in a 40hp Stearns on May 30, 1910. The five-mile race was a "free-for-all" run which Reed completed in 8 minutes, 33⁴/₅ seconds. The winged-wheel design on the base of the trophy is of importance as it figured prominently in most American and French races of the period.

"Los Angeles MotorDrome Trophy"

Dieges and Clust Jewelers. Bronze, 22 x 19½; America. *(right)* This was the first trophy presented at the inaugural meet of the MotorDrome, April 8-17, 1910. Ray Harroun won this trophy in a Marmon "32" stock car. He drove the required 100 miles in 78 minutes, 21.9 seconds averaging 78.6 mph without any pit stops, establishing a world record.

"First Indianapolis 500 - Second Prize Trophy"

Unsigned. Bronze, 21 x 11½; America, 1911. This trophy was presented to Ralph Mulford for placing second. Due to a breakdown of the automatic timing system during the race, inexperienced employees took over timekeeping operations. The race was contested by Mulford, who believed that he was shortchanged at least a full lap on the ledger. After all-night reviews and discussions of the racing data, speedway authorities still awarded first place to Ray Harroun in his Marmon. To this day, there is still debate and discussion about who really won the First Indianapolis 500.

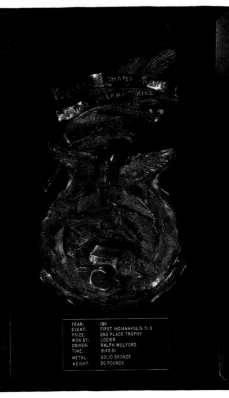

"Figueria-Lisbon Trophy"

Unsigned. Alloy and silver, 14 x 10; Portugal, 1909. The race was held between these two cities on October 27, 1909: the first place trophy is a medallion made of a metal alloy in bas relief. It sits within an ornate silver frame.

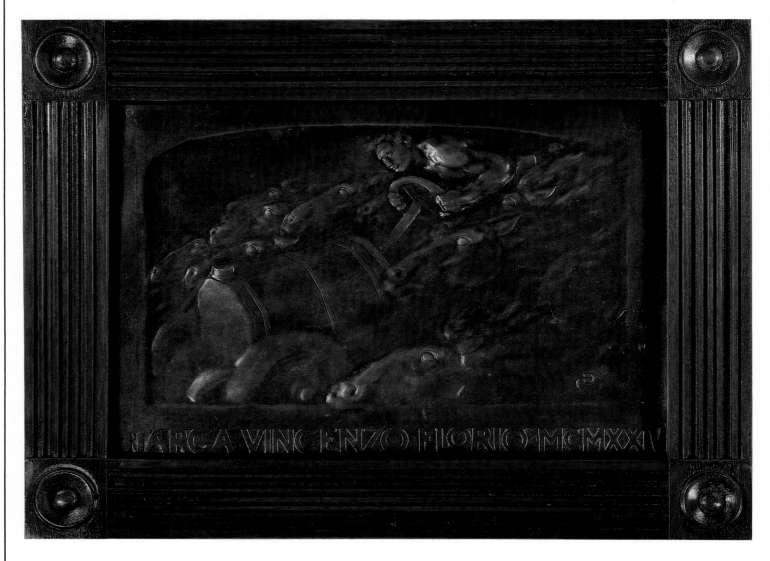

Left: Domenico Cambellotti. Bronze, 11 x 16¾; Italy, 1924. Right: Henri Dropsy (1885-1942). Silver, 21¼ x 16⅜; Italy, 1926. Vincenzo Florio, an avid motorist whose wealth came from the growing and processing of grapes to produce Marsala wine, sponsored the Coppa Florio Cup at Brescia beginning in 1904 and the Targa Florio series of races over various long circuits around the island of Sicily beginning in 1906. Florio sought artists to create appropriate trophies for the races and the first Coppa Florio trophy commission was given to Polak Aine (see page 139), while the first Targa Florio trophy was commissioned to Réne Lalique. Lalique created a rectangular "targa" plaque, the word used in Italy for the "license plate" on motor vehicles. His work depicted the race car with driver and mechanic in bas relief speeding down a road bordered by wildflowers, underneath a flock of swallows. The flowers and bird were highlighted with enamels. Lalique produced the plaques until 1907 when his artistic interest turned to glass.

Beginning in 1908, the plaques were designed and cast by Cambellotti, who produced the third-place prize won by Bordino in 1924 (left) and who continued to produce plaques until 1925.

The honor was then passed to Dropsy, who produced his first plaque for the race of 1926 (right), which was won by Costantini in a Type-35 Bugatti. Bugatti cars also took second and third. This plaque was held by the Bugatti family before it was given to the winner, Constantini. Dropsy captured the movement of man, machine and animal as they pass through the environment at speed. He studied under Thomas, Patey and Injalbert, all prominent artists in France during the late 19th and early 20th centuries. He was later a member of the Society of the Institute of French Artists and was knighted in the French Legion of Honor.

TARGA FLORIO 1926

1º COSTANTINI
2º MINOIA
3º GOUX

3
CERAMICS

THE CREATION and decoration of ceramic objects are among the most ancient arts in the world. Since ceramics are made of clay, materials to create such objects were available to prehistoric cultures; early humans used the same basic process of construction for thousands of years. A higher level of sophistication in the development and decoration of ceramics occurred in the Egyptian, Greek and Roman cultures. More recently, through archaeological findings, the chronological development of the art in these cultures has been compared to that of production in China.

The Chinese had strong ceramic traditions which evolved concurrently with the Mediterranean cultures. China passed these folkways to the eight islands today known as Japan. The transfer of sophisticated ceramic techniques to Western Europe can be traced to early Mediterranean land and sea trade routes established by Marco Polo in the late Thirteenth century.

The mass production of ceramics was highly refined by the time the automobile emerged on the scene. It was quite easy to mass produce the ''white blanks'' of molded plates or vessels, upon which the artist could place an automotive image. Germany, France and England had the artisan skills and the natural resources to produce the objects. These nations also were primarily responsible for the emerging technology of automotive development, so that artists could see the ''machine'' firsthand, something that was not available to their Oriental counterparts and obviously reflected in the final image.

Highly publicized and glamorized early road races in these nations also drew the attention of the general public, creating a market for items that were simply produced to sell as mementos of various events. Other objects, more highly detailed and sophisticated, were produced as gifts and awards for drivers, racing teams, car manufacturers and related sponsors. The importation of ceramic products for these same purposes to Europe or America, from countries in other parts of the world, such as the Orient, would not occur on any grand scale until after the turn of the century, when countries like Japan became industrialized.

To explain the objects presented in this chapter, a general overview of the subject is necessary. To create such art objects, clays are extracted from natural deposits which are found worldwide.

Egg Caricatures

G. LeGesch. Ceramic, 4¼ x 4⅜; France, ca. 1896. The French city-to-city races of 1896-97 brought rapid progress to the technological development of the automobile, yet the public was not willing to accept the invention, because of its lack of endurance and reliability. These factors were captured, partially out of cynicism, by the artist who designed and created objects for promotional purposes. Attributed to the artisan/ceramicist G. LeGesch, these caricature egg cups clearly reflect the fragility of the motor car at that time. Sold as souvenirs as early as the Paris-Marseilles-Paris Race of 1896, and definitely at the Paris-Trouville Race of August, 1897, few of the thousands produced survive to date. Left: biscuit egg cup highlighted with stains; above: china egg cup with blue underglaze.

Types of clay determine whether they will be used for porcelain, stoneware, earthenware or red earthenware products. Most ceramic businesses, for obvious reasons, located their operations near such deposits. From Osaka, Japan to Roseville, Ohio, countless companies produced objects for use or enjoyment. The quality of clay in the region oftentimes built company reputations, as exemplified through the blessings of Mother Nature in Cornwall, England, where some of the finest deposits of white clay (also called Kaolin) in the world are found. Few of these clays were left alone as mined from the earth. They, together with other types of clay, fluxes and extender materials such as sand or ''grog,'' were combined to form the clay body used by the potter. The composition of this clay body was determined by practical considerations such as firing temperatures, desired color of product, hardness and how the object was to be formed — whether it be molded, ''thrown'' on a potter's wheel or modelled. Once the artisan made the object, it would be decorated with colored clay coatings (slips) and carved (incised) before drying. Upon drying, the object would be fired in a kiln and left natural color or stained with metal oxides. This non-shiny finish is called ''biscuit'' or more often ''bisque.'' Delicate objects hardened by this first firing can be decorated more easily with other colored glazes. A glaze is a combination of silica, flux and alumina and may be clear, or colored with small additions of metallic oxides.

Most of the automotive art objects presented in this chapter are glazed. While many were for general sale, others were created as presentation objects or as competition trophies. Premier examples of sculptural objects in this section are exemplified in the works of Mariel Temporal and Emile De Coeur. Classic examples of sculpted/molded combinations are represented by the Amphora Company and the Rorning Company. The global use of molds are presented with the Royal Doulton ''Motorists'' series and the Roseville ''Tourist'' series.

The objects depicted in this section reflect the use of clay processes by artists in creating a lasting impression of the emerging automotive age. Prevailing artistic movements and their lingering influences in the field of ceramics seemed of less consequence than that of the ''fine arts'' such as painting and sculpture. Persons working with clay were more removed from the academic schools of influence and bound to traditions of object-making as opposed to art-making.

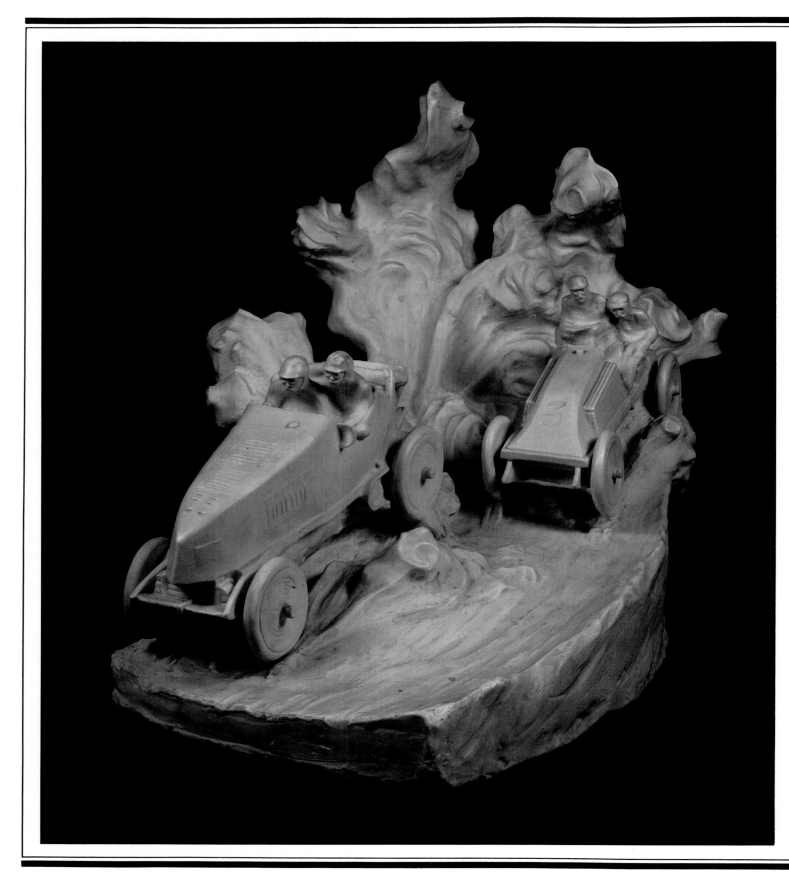

"The Paris-Madrid Race, 1903"

Mariel Temporal. Porcelain, 15 x 14; France, ca. 1903. Sunday, May 24, 1903 will always be remembered as one of the most tragic and bizarre days in the history of auto racing: the day of the Paris-Madrid Race. More than 130 vehicles began the race at Versailles and by the time they reached Bordeaux, some four drivers and mechanics, one soldier and one child had been killed. Five other drivers or mechanics were critically injured, and at least two dozen other drivers, mechanics or spectators received lesser injuries.

Severe heat and dust, large and enthusiastic spectator crowds, inefficient marshalling by authorities and a lack of barriers all contributed to this disastrous event, which immediately become known as the "Race of Death."

The race was halted by the French and Spanish governments at Bordeaux, where Gabriel in his streamlined Mors was awarded first place, having averaged 65.3 mph. Louis Renault came in second for the overall race, and placed first in the light car division, with an average speed of 62.3 mph. Tragically, Renault's brother Marcel struck a drain at the side of the road at the village of Couhe-Verac, causing his car to swing around twice and land on him. He died shortly thereafter.

Mariel Temporal was one of a score of artists commissioned by the participating governments to provide trophies and prizes that were to have been awarded after the finish at Madrid. When the official winners were declared at Bordeaux, Temporal meticulously created this hand-formed and carved porcelain. Temporal captures the anxiety and tension of the racers, and the speed and energy of their cars. In the work, Gabriel's car is shown leading, with Louis Renault alongside. A glaze had been used for highlighting, while the remainder of the body is in flat finish.

Cherub and Goddess

China, 9⅝ x 9 ¼; Germany, ca. 1897. This piece is china with underglaze stain and traces of gold luster. It depicts the male cherub guiding the Goddess of Victory in the motor car. The car itself is fashioned after the French-made Panhard of the 1893-1897 period, and the overall artistic style is Symbolist/Art Nouveau, probably based on a drawing made by Daniel Dupuis for the Automobile Club of France around 1893.

Vases

Bone china, 5¼ x 5½; Germany, ca. 1899. This pair of flower vases of male and female motorists is highlighted with stain.

Flower Vases

Germany and France, ca. 1902. These delicate vases, similar in style to the Gordon Bennett trophy for automobile racing, were made in molds and hand-decorated with an underglaze highlighted with gold paint. Marked "D.E.P.," the "white blanks" were probably made in Germany with finishes applied in France. Large piece: china, 8⅛ x 9; small piece: biscuit, 5 x 5½.

"The Gordon Bennett Trophy"

After Andre Aucoc. Bone china, 11¼ x 11⅝ France, ca. 1904. The Gordon Bennett Cup originated in America, when automaker Alexander Winton made a successful run from New York to Cleveland in the summer of 1899, averaging 17.6 mph. When Winton heard of Fernand Charron's victory in the Automobile Club of France's Paris-Bordeaux race in May that year, he challenged Charron to a match over the impressive distance of 1000 miles. Charron accepted the challenge and even deposited 20,000 francs at the Paris office of the *New York Herald* as a sign of his good faith. Even though Charron's car was much more likely than Winton's to complete the race, the idea of a Franco-American competition seemed to arouse the public. The race was never held because a month later, James Gordon Bennett, owner and publisher of the *Herald*, expanded the idea and proposed a race in which teams from the national motoring clubs of France, Germany, Great Britain, Belgium, Austria, Switzerland, Italy and the United States would compete for the prize. The French newspapers heralded the coming of the "Coupe Internationale." W.F. Bradley, the pioneer motoring journalist at the *Herald*, on the other hand, publicized it as the "Gordon Bennett Race." Bennett always played down the fact that the race was named after him, wanting it to be called "the Columbia Cup." Although a founding member of the Automobile Club of France, Bennett was not an avid motorist, preferring the challenge of sailing. He would avoid riding in a motor car, never learned to drive and always attended events in a "coach and four."
At the instigation of the Chevalier Rene de Knyff, the Marquis de Dion and Baron de Zuylen, Bennett initiated a search for an artist to create and execute "a valuable objet d'art" as the racing trophy. He found and commissioned Andre Aucoc, the well-known Paris

silversmith, to undertake the task. Because of his long association with the A.C.F., Bennett specified that the new sculpture reflect the design of the medallion created for that body a decade before. Depicting the Genius of Progress steering a Panhard-inspired motor car while the Goddess of Victory stands upon the seat waiting to hand over the palm to the winner, Aucoc created a Rococo masterpiece of silver. The trophy is still owned and exhibited by the A.C.F. in Paris. The design was released by Aucoc to Gordon Bennett in late 1899.
Since all of the trophies for race car owners, drivers and mechanics could not be cast in silver, Aucoc, at Bennett's

request, oversaw the production of at least a score of high quality china versions of his masterwork. A number of these were of bone china, using underglaze, overglaze, gold enamel and decals for highlighting. Others of biscuit finish utilized stains for highlights. Each known in existence differs from all the others, due to the creativity of the artisans who added the final touches. Other pieces of the same design, but of lesser quality, were produced and given to other early participants in the competition *(right)* and in at least one case, the same piece had Mercury *(below)* placed in the seat to accompany the Goddess of Victory; but this is a later alteration.

Children's Sipping Cup

China, 3½ x 3; America. P.S. Heinl, owner of a general store in Wisconsin, ordered these promotional cups imprinted with the photographic image of his son in a pedal car.

Vases

Bone china, 6 x 7⅜; Germany, ca. 1898. *(left and below)* These flower vases, made of bone china with a biscuit finish and stain, are indicative of turn-of-the-century style.

"Monsieur et Madam Pussy"

Biscuit, 5 x 4⅞; ca. 1900. *(above)* One of numerous condiment and candy containers produced from 1900 until 1905, the medium is biscuit decorated with fired stains.

Decorated Vase

Earthenware with transfer print, 8⅞ x 2⅛; Germany, ca. 1900. *(left)* This rare and delicate vase with a female driver was made to accompany a tea set.

Nodders

Biscuit, 7⅝ x 3; Germany, ca. 1900. "Nodders" were highly favored by children and collectors at the turn-of-the century because they offered articulated movement of parts, but did not have any breakable mechanisms. This biscuit man and woman in motoring garb were made in Germany shortly after 1900, and are highlighted with gold-metal luster paint.

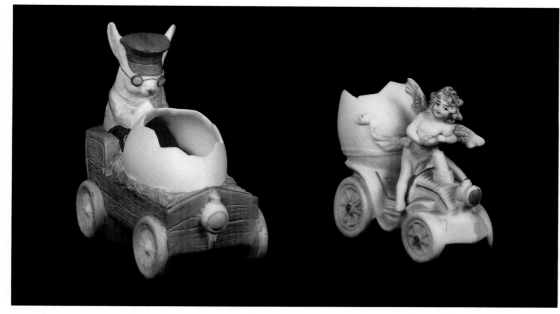

Egg Cup and Cherub

Biscuit with stain; Germany, ca. 1902. *(above)* A rabbit egg cup sits beside a cherub driving a vehicle. Egg cup: 4 x 4; cherub: 3⅛ x 3⅝.

"Doggie Chauffeur"

Earthenware with overglaze and enamel highlight, 4¼ x 4¼; Germany, ca. 1902. *(above right)* Condiment dish.

Egg Cars

Biscuit, Germany and France, ca. 1902. *(right)* The "white blanks" for these two novelty pieces were probably made in Germany with the stain and gold luster highlighting added in France. Large piece: 5 x 5½; small piece: 3⅞ x 4½.

Bric-a-Brac

China and biscuit, 1¾ - 4⅜ x 1½ - 2⅝; Europe ca. 1900. *(left)* A variety of miniature molded china and biscuit "bric-a-brac" characters including a black chauffeur, a birthday car, a Gordon Bennett racer and a man in an accident.

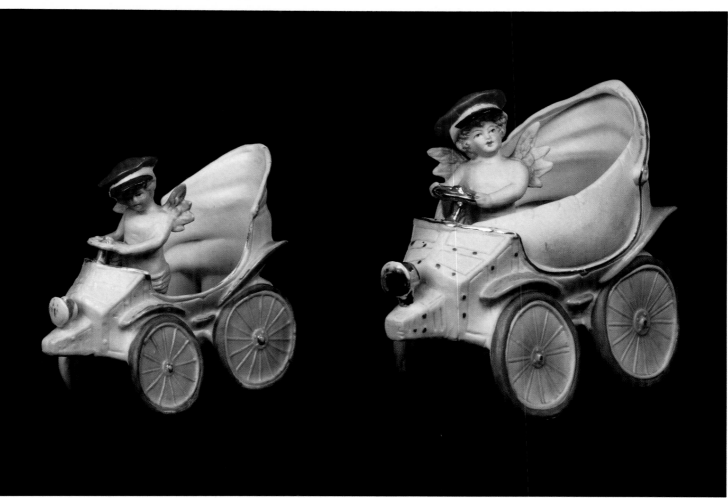

"Club Del Buongustaio"

Bessi. Porcelain, 16 x 20; Italy, ca. 1902. A Fiat motor car is featured in the center of this advertising sign for ''The Good Time Club.''

"Paris to Madrid—1903"

Emile DeCoeur. Earthenware, 6¾ x 10⅝; France, ca. 1908. Emile DeCoeur was commissioned in 1908 to produce five of these objects for Paul Moreau-Vauthier, who was the sculptor for the original bronze in 1903. DeCoeur was a French ceramicist who created this work in two pieces, the body of the race car separating to expose an oblong cigarette or candy compartment. Made of earthenware, the object is glazed inside with a low-luster glaze finish on the exterior. The car represents the Mors driven by Gabriel in the race and is fifth of an edition believed to number five. The remaining four have never been found.

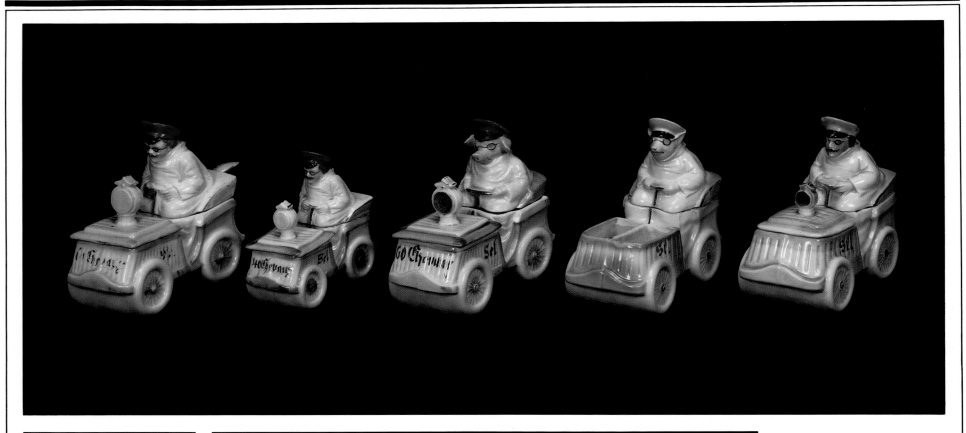

Condiment Sets

Glazed china, 3½ - 5¼ x 3⅝ - 5⅛; Europe ca. 1903. Many people who enjoyed motor car racing at the turn-of-the-century had a favorite car and/or driver. Condiment sets with automotive shapes were mass-produced and sold on the day of the race. As items were bought, the vendor would paint the name of the race or driver on the object according to the customer's request. A "Road Hog" character at the wheel would indicate German manufacture. All of the objects are glazed china with overglaze gold luster and underglaze highlights.

Right: a condiment set from the Paris-Berlin Race of 1901, which commemorates Grus in his Renault passing through the outskirts of Eiselburg, Germany. Object on right is unpainted.

Above: Condiment sets from 1901 through the Paris-Madrid race of 1903.

"Road Hog"

China, 5¼ x 6⅛; Germany, ca. 1903. (above) This unusually large condiment set had movable wheels and was produced to reflect city-to-city races. It features underglazed highlights with gold luster.

Souvenir Set

Left to right:

Bud Vase. Earthenware, 4½ x 4; Germany, ca. 1904.

Sipping Cup. China, 2½ x 2; Germany, ca. 1904.

Bob-bob Dish. Earthenware, 1¼ x 4½; Germany, ca. 1904.

Plates

Upper left: Lyi. China, 11⅜ d.; France, ca. 1904. Lyi painted this ornate Panhard touring car at the Flambeau Company's factory in Limoges, France.

Upper right: China, 11⅝; Germany, ca. 1904. "ST" pottery of Bavaria produced this vivid, gilt-edged image of a 1904 10hp Rolls-Royce.

Bottom: "The Voyage." Phignony. China, 14½. Phignony, during a later period, painted this piece as part of a series called "La Belle Epoque" for the Longway Company. The work is number 553 in an edition of 1000, which may have never been completed.

Race car container

China, 3⅜ x 6⅞; France, ca. 1903. A unique object, made of china that uses colors and luster for detailing and is coated with a clear glaze inside and out. The hood cover is missing and the driver covers a compartment.

STEINS

Steins

Fine quality steins have been produced for societies, guilds and organizations for the last 150 years. Such ceramic objects were designed by artisans working for pottery companies, many of which were located in and around the regions of Bavaria and Wurtemberg, Germany. Most of the pieces shown were cast white earthenware with raised images and separately applied parts, such as handles. Artisans experienced in a wide variety of glazing techniques applied the enamels and luster to the work. Textural highlighting of the pieces were also carved or incised by hand.

Opposite page, left to right:

8 x 7; Germany, ca. 1904. This colorful one-litre stein portrays two children reporting a "speeder" to the constable, while the farmer's wife waves her broom at the motorist. A "3" is found on the hood of the car attached to the lid, while "7001" is designated on the license plate. An artisan with the initials "K.O.G." produced the vessel.

14¾ x 6½, ca. 1907. This two-litre stein depicts a couple looking on as their chauffeur stops the car to converse with a gypsy.

6¾ x 5½, date unknown. A half-liter, salt-fired stein that depicts an image bearing a resemblance to reliefs created by Dropsy for the Targa Florio Races that were staged in Italy during the post World War I period. The symbolic eagle of the Deutschland is recessed on the lid; the piece also has the initials "A.D.A.C." (Allgemeiner Deutsche Automobil Club).

Above, left to right:

9¼ x 6¼; Germany, ca. 1909. An early one-liter stein with two Germanic inscriptions that mean "Search in the future for your fondest desire- Hurry through the World in an automobile" and "Oh son- the moments of driving in the car with you are Happiness." The lid has the emblem and initials of the A.D.A.C. inscribed.

9 ¼ x 6¼; Germany, ca. 1910. A half-liter stein sold as a souvenir of Niagara Falls, Canada.

8½ x 5; Germany, ca. 1908. Two chauffeured couples touring toward Dresden are found on the image of this one-liter stein.

9 x 5½; Germany, ca. 1924. One-liter salt-glaze finish stein portraying a lady holding "ale" in steins while her husband drives the car.

Half-liter Stein

Earthenware, 6½ x 3½; Germany, ca. 1910.

Vases

Four mass-produced vessels showing the disruption of the motor car in rural life. Above, left to right:

M. Biaise. China, 6⅛ x 3¼; France, ca. 1903. This features an early motor car in motion, scaring a child and two geese.

China with transfer print, 5 ⅝ x 3⅜; Germany, ca. 1904. Another mass-produced vase, this one depicts a chauffeur and a lady in a motor car that is scaring a car and chickens.

M. Biais. Earthenware, 4 x 2¾; France, ca. 1900. Both of these pieces portray domestic animals being frightened by racing cars. The one on the right is stamped "Porcelaine Opaque de Gien" for marketing purposes, but is, in fact, earthenware, like its mate. Produced in the region surrounding Gien, this utilitarian line found a ready market in nearby Paris.

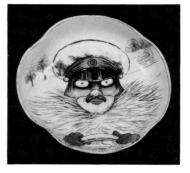

Ashtrays

Molded china with transfer print, 4¾ d.; Germany, ca. 1904. A "his and hers" set of colored ashtrays, with drawings like those of artist Edward Gorey.

Flower Vase

Bone china, 8 x 8¾; Germany,
ca. 1904. The lady drives the
gentleman in this delightful
vase, which is highlighted with
overglaze.

The "Tourist" Series

Ceramic; America, ca. 1906. The Roseville Pottery Company, with headquarters in Zanesville, Ohio, produced millions of pottery pieces during the years of 1898-1954. Shortly after 1900, the company opened a sales office on Madison Avenue in New York City. During a visit to the New York office, the art director heard a story about the Vanderbilt and Astor families. Since the mid-Eighteen-seventies, the Vanderbilt family had painted its carriages maroon; the Astors painted theirs blue. Both continued this color tradition as they purchased motorcars for family and business. Thinking that a motoring series would sell well in the New York market, and offering both family colors, the "Tourist" series was created and sold from 1906-1916. An estimated 400,000 molded off-white pieces were produced during that time. Painted with cream-colored slip for background, transfer print landscape scenes were applied and then hand-painted with a palette that captures detail in rich maroons, mild oranges and varied greens. The bands are underglazed to add contrast to the pieces. Most known works feature maroon cars, blue car pieces being extremely rare. Stories prevail of the "Tourist" band on a green Chloron piece produced by Roseville and sold at auction in the Fifties, but photos, auction records and location have never been substantiated. Approximately 29 different shapes and/or sizes of objects were in the line, depicting four different motoring scenes. Usually, two vehicles are found on the larger objects, and one on smaller pieces. Less than 500 examples are believed to have survived.

Left: A large jardiniere on pedestal base 12 x 15; pedestal base 21 x 12.

Above: Flower vases: small 7½ x 5⅛; medium 9¼ x 6¼; large 12¼ x 7¼.

Right: Umbrella stand 22½ x 9¾.

Lower right: Small jardiniere 7 x 8½; medium jardiniere 10 x 12¾.

Lower left: Small flower box 7 x 13¼.

"The Racer"

Adrien-Pierre Dalpayrat. Ceramic, 4½ x 14; France, ca. 1903. Dalpayrat was born in 1844 at Limoges, France. For generations, his family was involved with the ceramics business and by 1900, he was one of the finest ceramicists in the country. That year, he was knighted into the Legion of Honor for his contributions to art. For his most desired pieces, Dalpayrat found and maintained a secret source of clay that had a high copper and cobalt content. After modeling the objects, he would apply an iron-oxide wash. On all or portions of his automotive works, he would then use a green glaze and allow it to run down over the work before firing at high temperatures. The results created a unique effect called "Rouge Dalpayrat," with reddish tones penetrating the green glaze. In "The Racer," Dalpayrat captures the speed of the early racing car, especially through the mud splashing along the side of the road.

Presentation Bowl

Earthenware, 3 x 5½; European, ca. 1905. Made of earthenware with overglaze and highlighted with gold-enamel, this bowl has a hole in the lid to allow for attachment of mementos relating to a particular event.

"The Motorists"

Royal Doulton; George Holdcroft. China; England, 1903-1913. Transfer print, a process invented and refined in the Seventeen-Fifties, allowed an outline image to be placed directly on the surface of a "white blank." Working to these outlines, an artist could produce hand-painted objects at an increased rate. This series, "The Motorists," was originally sketched by George Holdcroft in about 1903 and was mass-produced through transfer print at the Doulton factory on Nile Street in Burslem, England. Doulton produced one of the finest industrial glazes in Europe at the time. Such clear glaze is found on these molded china objects, which were hand-painted over the transfer print. These utilitarian objects were produced and marketed between 1903 and 1913, with the greatest production being in the last two years. Through exposure at the great international exhibitions of the period, Royal Doulton exchanged its technology and initiated international trade for such products. It is believed the company showed these designs and wares for the first time at the St. Louis Exhibition of 1904. The major markets for this series were England, Germany, France and the United States. Eight scenes were available in the series: "After The Run," "A Horse, A Horse," "Blood Money," "Deaf," "Itch yer on Guv'nor?" (Can I find you a tow, sir?), "Nerve Tonic," "Room For One" and "The New and The Old."

Dimensions of the pieces in "The Motorists" set are as follows (height, except where indicated): large pitchers for beer steins 14½; serving dishes, large 4 x 9, small 4 x 8; serving platters 12⅝ d.; dinner plates, large 10⅜ d., small 9⅝ d.; dinner mugs, large 5¾, small 5½; spitton 7; flower vase 9¼; biscuit jar/cover 8; pitchers (largest to smallest) 7½, 6¾, 6, and 5¼.

Occupation Shaving Mugs

Bone china, 3 - 4 x 4¼ - 5; America. A wonderful and broad scope collection of occupational mugs that could be found in the neighborhood barber shop before World War I. White mug blanks made in Germany were purchased by the patron from the barber; then a local artist would paint the name of the patron and the nature of his business in the scene found on the mug. Found in this collection are individuals who were motor car builders, bankers, lawyers and other types of business personages who used the automobile in their daily work or for social pleasure.

"The Racers" Mug

Bone china, 3½ x 4¾; Germany, ca. 1907. The bone china "blank" was manufactured in Germany, then exported to the United States, where a local artisan painted the cars and drivers on the object. This piece, titled "The Racers," honored a certain Frank LeRusse. This is considered one of the rarest known vessels of this type, due to the quality of art work and the image subject, which depicts two racing cars in the scene.

Plates

Earthenware, 11-12 d.; France, ca. 1905. Molded white earthenware plates were popular in promoting the image of the automobile inexpensively. Using colored transfer prints, little hand-painting was needed and these "chargers" were an easy product for small potteries to produce and sell.

Top left: Signed "BFK," the caption on this plate reads "Oh! Biddy! A pretty one for Christmas!!"

Top right: A large serving plate painted by E. Geles in France carries the legend "John, would you please hurry up - my train leaves in 7 minutes."

Lower center: This plate, painted by Obert and manufactured by the "K & G" pottery firm, is based upon Montaut's lithograph of a Clement Bayard car in the Gordon Bennett race of 1905.

Flasks

Above, left:
China, 2¾ x 5½; Germany, ca. 1906. A product of the Schaffer-Vader Company, the ''spirit'' china flask was mass produced as a publicity handout, in this case by a tire company in Akron, Ohio.

Above, middle and right:
China, 7¼ x 2⅛; Europe, ca. 1906. The two delightful figures could be found in the French and English markets, with the lady sporting a stylish ''Brighton'' double-breasted longcoat (biscuit with stain highlights) and the gentleman a single-breasted ''Drykner'' driving jacket (biscuit with stain highlights). Note the detailed design pattern found in the ''leggings'' worn by the gentleman. Both garbs are still worn by members of the veteran car organization ''Club de Teufs-Teufs'' during tours.

Desktop Touring Car

China, 8½ x 18½; Germany, ca. 1905. *(left)* This decorative art table/desk object was made by the Furster Company. The bonnet had vertical louvers, as on French cars, but the chain drive cover box was introduced by German automobile companies as a safety feature on their touring cars, so it is hard to determine what kind of car it is. A later application of lacquer was added to portions of the work, but was done poorly and is chipping due to poor bonding and shrinkage.

"Roosevelt Bears"

Earthenware, 7¼-10¼; America, ca. 1905. The Roosevelt Bears became very popular after Theodore Roosevelt was inaugurated as President for the second time in 1905. Each scene features a historical, technological or personal event in which Roosevelt participated. The automobile scene commemorates Roosevelt as the first President to use an automobile, a White Steamer, as the official mode of transportation for the White House. The scene of the "Roosevelt Bears Take an Auto Ride" is one of 16 found on the pitcher. Some other scene titles are the Roosevelt Bears ". . . at Harvard," ". . . in a balloon," and ". . . at Plymouth Rock." The pieces are molded, with the scenes transfer-printed. Hand-painted underglaze has been used to highlight the rim, base and handle of pitcher. A sponge and brush were used to apply an overglaze gold luster. The Buffalo Pottery Company of Buffalo, New York, copyrighted and produced the series, with greatest sales of the line from 1905 through early 1908, T.R.'s heyday years.

Pipe Holders

China, 5⅛ - 6¾; Germany, ca. 1922. *(left)* These pipe holders are attributed to an unknown German manufacturer. Made of china with underglaze, clear glaze and highlighted with overglaze colors, they are marked "D.R.G.M. - B.E.S. Beschutz," which signifies a registered trademark for the design.

"Nodders"

Porcelain, 6 x 3; Germany, ca. 1907. These "nodder" figurines portray male and female motorists wearing "Double-breasted Chesterfield" and "Adderly" coats respectively. These are made of molded porcelain with overglaze and enamel highlights.

"Out of Gas"

China, 11 x 6¼; Austria, ca. 1905. This pitcher is modelled as a portly lady in motoring garb. Marked "AE GESSTZICH," the object is made of china with underglaze and highlighted with gold paint enamel.

Banks and Candy Containers

China, 5⅛-6 x 6¾-8½; Germany, ca. 1906. Produced of china with underglaze and gold highlights, this variety of banks and candy containers was originally produced around 1906, though later reproductions were made in the early Twenties and early Forties.

Mercedes Racing Car

Rornig. Earthenware, 10¾ x 22⅜; Austria, 1908. Under the technical consultation of Emil Adam, a highly respected professor of ceramic chemistry, the Kunstkeramischen Fabrik A. Forster Company of Austria began to develop innovative shape and pattern designs as early as 1902. One of Adam's greatest contributions to the company was his experimentation with finishes on various types of clay bases. Rornig created this 120bhp Mercedes racing car in an edition of 500 to commemorate the model's victory in the French Grand Prix of 1908. They were distributed worldwide as showroom ornaments and gifts. Made of a white earthenware, the car body was cast, with other parts such as the horn, fenders and steering wheel being modeled by hand. Shading is given to the object through expert use of underglaze coloring, which, when covered with a clear glaze, accentuates the textural nature of the piece. A blue shading has also been reported on pieces. Such application of the finish would stem from Professor Adam's advice. Adding electrical headlights and a spring driven clock in the hand-incised grid of the radiator was all part of the creativity and success of the company. The Forster firm changed owners in late 1908.

"Motorcar Ware"

China; England, ca. 1909. Produced on a limited scale, this Motorcar Ware moustache sipping cup and creamer are rare examples of the 60 piece set. The creamer measures 3⅛ x 4, the sipping cup is 4⅛ x 5¼.

"Easter Egg Auto"

China, 7 x 9½; French, date unknown. Underglaze and gold enamel highlight this ornate candy dish.

Steins

Royal Doulton. Earthenware, 7⅛ x 5; England, ca. 1908. This rare set of prototype steins is molded of white earthenware, with the hat brim outlined in blue underglaze. A silver band was added around the upper lip. The odd color of the finish is attributed to Cuthbert Bailey, a colleague of Henry Doulton who led the company's experimentation with high heat coloration finishes.

Dining Table Dish

China, 7³/₈ x 13¹/₂; ca. 1910. Mints, toothpicks and flowers adorned this colorful container, used at the dinner table.

Amphora Figurines

Earthenware, 13⁵/₈ x 6; Bohemia, ca. 1910. The Amphora Works was established in 1892 at Turn (Trnovany), then in Bohemia. While most of their works were high quality porcelain, they also produced exquisite white earthenware products. In 1893, the company won artistic prizes in competitions from Antwerp to Chicago. With the seemingly endless conflicts that were occurring in the Austro-Hungarian Empire at the time, the company changed factory locations in response to the various political partitionings of the region. This rare, highly-defined pair of motorists attired in the driving fashion of the day justifies Amphora's reputation for exotic detail and eccentric outlines (note the open front of the lady's Adderly styled coat). Made from molds, these objects were hand-painted with underglaze, colored glazes and overglaze enamels to give a rich, colorful finish.

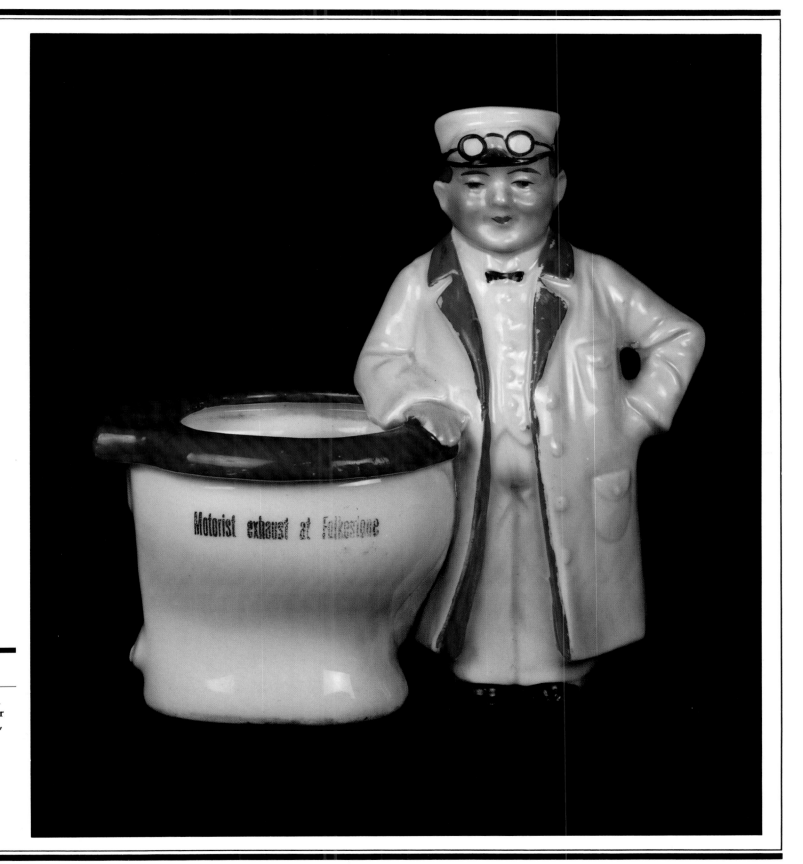

"Motorist Exhaust at Folkestone"

China, 5¼ x 5½; England, ca. 1912. This humorous souvenir market item is made of china, underglazed with applied overglaze enamels.

Teapots

China, 4¼ x 8½; England, ca. 1927. These molded china teapots were produced in England by Sadler, Ltd. and in America by Hall's Superior Quality Kitchenware, Co., from 1927 through the mid-Thirties. Sadler pots were of bright colors with metal luster highlights and had a license plate signature of "OKT42." Sadler also produced creamer, sugar and condiment sets for its line. The English company's pots are marked with registered patent number 820236. Hall's pots were produced in more subtle tones, again using enamel highlights. It coded the product line according to color (i.e. black was 05030P, blue was 0523P and so on). Molded reproductions of these teapots have been produced in England throughout the Eighties, but such copies lack any registration numbers.

Dinnerware

Villeroy and Boch. China; Germany, ca. 1920. Villeroy and Boch produced a motoring dinner series in the late Twenties at its Dresden, Germany factory, which was closed after severe damage from Allied bombing in World War II. The objects are china with colored slip highlights. Transfer stencil is used for the car itself, details being applied by hand in brown, green and white. The serving platter (14 d.), dinner plate (12½ d.), drinking cup (4½ x 3⅜) and two cracker decanters (7¼ x 5) took on a rich look after the final clear glaze was applied and dried.

Perfume Atomizer

Porcelain, 4⅜ x 11¼; France, 1925. Produced by the Aladdin Company in Paris, these perfumers were in vogue for a short time in the mid-Twenties. Electric headlamps created heat which dissipated perfume placed in a hollow where the hood ornament was found. The car, possibly inspired by the 1100 cc. Amilcar, is typical of the French racing voiturette or sports car characteristic the insouciant 1920-27 period. The piece is a wonderful example of Art Deco styling, using overglaze enamel for coloration and gold overglaze to suggest speed and motion.

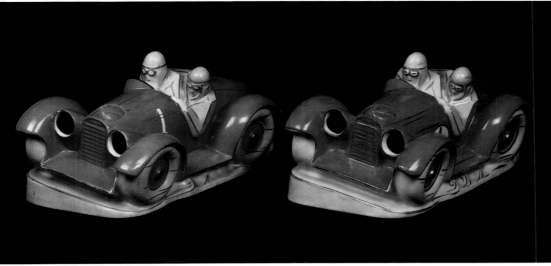

Floaters

Tobacco humidors have been very popular throughout the decades and many vessels were created in the image of the male motorist in appropriate headgear.

At left, left: Biscuit, 3 x 4½; Germany. Produced by the artist "TS," who used dark stain on the biscuit humidor to accomplish the coloring effect.

At left, right: Artist "CH" applied overglaze to the china object to present a more colorful effect. Both pieces are marked "8254," with the biscuit piece being #50 in the edition.

Humidor

China, 6 x 7; Austria, ca. 1919. *(left)* A rare humidor capturing the intensity, integrity and commitment of the early motorist. Made of china with underglaze and overglaze highlights.

"The Chauffeur"

Earthenware, 7½ x 5; Austria, ca. 1910. *(above)* A hand-painted, earthenware tobacco humidor with underglaze and marked with "J.M."

"The Lady Motorist"

Earthenware, 11 x 4¼; Austria, ca. 1910. A hand-painted molded earthenware tobacco humidor, marked "B.A." A delightful depiction.

HUMIDORS

Peko-styled Humidors

China, 4½ d.; Germany, ca. 1925. Obviously produced from the male chauffeur images found on the prints created by Peko (see page 86 of Chapter One), these molded humidors were caricature portrayals of motorists during the period.

Left to right: The first two are of the same mold (# 9528), but their color and cigar size varies. They are numbers 34 and 49 of the edition respectively. The next wear English garb with a frowning face, perhaps due to the notoriety of English weather.

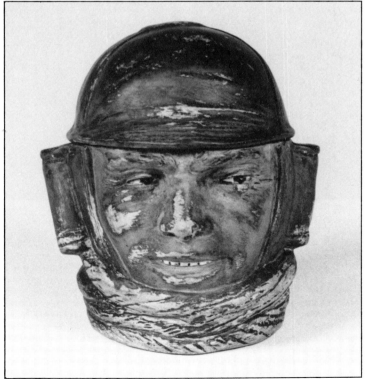

Motoring Humidor

Earthenware, 6 x 5; Germany, ca. 1912. *(left)*

Humidor

Molded china, 5 x 6; Germany, ca. 1920. This humidor was manufactured in Germany shortly after World War I, marked ''WS&S'' on production line number 3337. The artist used underglaze, then covered the object with clear glaze to produce the coloring effects.

Nipponware

Ceramic; Japan, ca. 1900's. The Japanese produced millions of ceramic objects for export during the late 19th century and early twentieth century. The "white blanks" produced at the factory were sent to a group of artisans, usually an entire community, for decoration and then returned to the factory for export. If you study the objects closely, you will recognize that quality "white blanks" were sometimes sent to poor decorators or vice versa, so one must be observant in assessing the overall object. Additionally, the automobile was a rare presence in Japanese society and many decorators had never seen the real thing, only pictures of what they were to reproduce. One notes the effect of this on the interpretation of the automobile as detailed on the objects in these photos.

The following objects were produced in Japan and exported to the United States after the turn-of-the-century, and are commonly referred to as "Nipponware." The name "Nippon" began to appear on Japanese products imported into America in 1891. This was a direct result of the McKinley Tariff Act, which required the country of origin to print its name on each object in English. The Japanese used their own word, which is "Nippon." This practice lasted for 30 years until 1921, when political influences caused the United States Treasury to declare that the English word "Japan" was to be used, since "Nippon" was a Japanese word.

Most of the automotive objects imported into the United States bear the "'M'-in-Wreath" mark, and were produced by Noritake. The "M" in the wreath mark stands for the Morimura Brothers in New York, the sole importers of Noritake in the United States at the time. Noting the vehicles represented, it is safe to assess that most of the pieces were probably decorated as early as 1905 through 1921.

Left: Lady's spittoon. Molded china; Japan. A lady's spittoon of molded china with full glaze on the inside and partially on the outside, highlighted with stain, underglazed colors and raised enamels. Stamped with "M."

Middle: Humidor. Molded china; Japan. This molded china humidor is glazed on the inside and bottom. The scenes are hand-painted with china paints and background colors are stained. This object is typical of decorative work produced in the Kaga Province of Japan.

Right: Lady's snuff box. Molded china, 2³⁄₈ x 2³⁄₄; Japan. A lady's snuff box of molded china, glazed inside and on outer opening. It has a stained background with scenes drawn in china paint. Raised enamels frame the painted areas.

Candy dish

Roby of Paris. Bone china, 4¹⁄₄ x 11³⁄₈; France, ca. 1926. (opposite) Decorated in red, black and gold enamels, this candy dish was one of the first French lines produced in the Art Deco style. (Note that the lid is missing.)

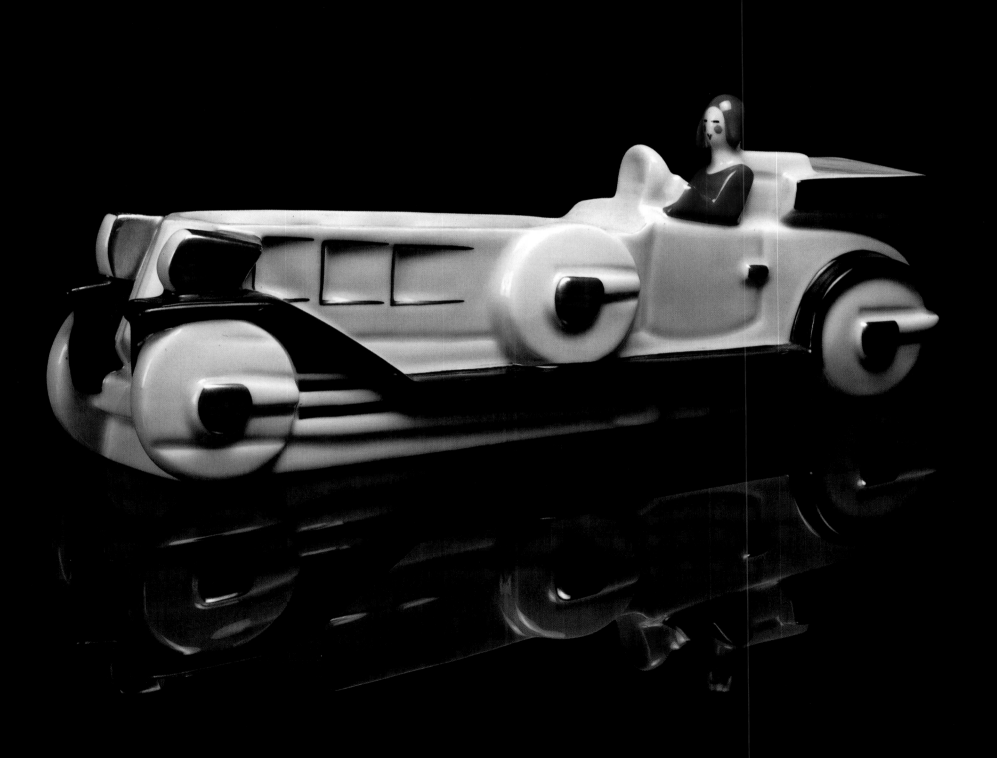

4
MIXED MEDIA

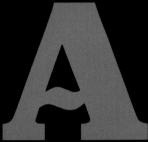

VARIETY OF MEDIA used by artists for interpreting and promoting the automobile with their art can be found in this section. Such materials were less often used in depicting the automobile than the media found in other sections, but each object is of equal importance in the ability of artists to present the automobile to a curious and interested world.

The largest number of objects given consideration in this section are made of marble, which has always been more extensively used by artists than any type of stone. Consisting of fine grains, marble was greater in stability and much easier to work with than stone such as igneous rock. Marble also is more durable and lasting in presentation, making it more appealing than minerals such as limestone. The closeness of the grain allows marble to be polished to a high finish, perhaps the greatest reason why it has been favored as a sculptural stone by artists since ancient Greek and Roman times. Perhaps the most outstanding automotive art object of marble in the world is the sculptural piece created by Charles Millard, titled "Coupe d'Atlas." Millard used "Escalette" stone mined in northern France for this work, which interprets the continued dominance of Nature, represented by the lion and lioness, above man and technology. Another outstanding work, rich in heavily veined coloring, is Antonio Giorgi's delightful bust of Elizabeth Junek, the young, vibrant, renowned Bugatti race driver of the nineteen-twenties.

As early as 2500 B.C., artists of the Egyptian VI Dynasty experimented with gypsum materials to produce death masks for kings and other members of royalty. By the late eighteenth century, these gypsum products would be commonly called "Plaster of Paris," a name derived by the rich deposits found near Paris and used by artists. Plaster of Paris has always been easy to mix, uncomplicated in casting, readily available for producing multiple copies, and highly favorable because of its low cost. Three-dimensional objects in many cases were first cast in this substance as study models with students of art history, allowing them to change or modify work before producing a final product. Such may have been the case in the creation of "Resta's Victory at Indianapolis" by Alexis Kow, who, along with an artist named

"Mercedes"

Unsigned. Plaster, 19½ x 8¼; Germany, ca. 1938. A rare, pre-World War II advertising figure used to promote the Mercedes coupe.

Jilsk, cooperatively created the work featuring a Peugeot race car from plaster around 1922. Shortly thereafter, Kow was commissioned by Peugeot to do other art work. Other exemplary works from plaster are that of Alfred-Jean Halou, whose arching goddess rises above her earthly domain in "L'Transportation," and LaFon Mollo's humorous "Auto Circuit" which captures the true essence and spirit of typical motoring tourists of the day.

Like marble and plaster, glass had it roots in ancient Mediterranean cultures. As early as 1906, glass was becoming more and more popular with artists in the automotive interpretations. Hard and durable, if handled with care, glass always has had magical qualities, particularly when held to the light or set in a window of bright sunlight. Each day and each changing weather condition allowed for glass images to be enjoyed and aesthetically appreciated by the owner or collector. For the artist/glassblower with knowledge of metal and metal oxide chemistry, the color formulas found in the art work could guarantee a lifetime of success in this field of art. The window using Walter Thor's "A La Recherche Du Contact" image is undoubtedly one of the most significant stained glass art objects of the automobile in existence from pre-World War I.

Francois Danton's masterful tapestry depicting the Goddess of Speed leading a De Dion-Bouton limousine through the French countryside represents one of the most labor intensive objects in art. Danton's use of the "basse lisse" technique in the production of his horizontal warp tapestry was basically the same used by his family ancestors when Louis XIV granted the town of Aubusson, France the designation of "Royal Manufactory of Tapestry" in 1665. Only the final quality of dying in the work changed significantly during the time between the Louis XIV period and Danton's work in 1906. A less difficult, but still striking image of American origins of this period's textiles, is the delightful fireplace screen created by Malcolm A. Strauss.

An immense amount of time and energy was expended by artists to produce these objects that hold the common theme of the automobile. As one views their images a century later, appreciation must be given to the fact that even though the automobile, a Twentieth century technological product of the Industrial Age served as the stimuli for their art, that the roots of their thoughts, processes, techniques and style came from non-industrial origins of a time long past.

"Traveller's Music Box"

Mixed materials, 4⅜ x 8⅝; Switzerland, ca. 1902. *(opposite)* The scenes on the box depict four young women on a motoring tour. This type of handcranked music box was given as a friendship gift and was played for entertainment at home or on tour.

Decorative Bowl

Unsigned. Crystal glass, 3¾ x 6½; England, ca. 1903. *(above)* An Edwardian gentleman stands next to his Napier-inspired motor car.

"Coupe Gordon Bennett"

Unsigned. Glass, 6½ x 5½; France, ca. 1903. *(above)* This Grecian-style, blue cobalt goblet has gold-and-white, hand-painted race cars and decorative braiding. The international color of blue, used herein, was assigned to France for the Gordon Bennett Race.

"The Lady Motorist"

Malcolm A. Strauss. Linen, 23 x 22½; America, ca. 1898. Strauss created this fireplace screen by stretching the linen, then sketching the outline of the image and applying dyes with sponges, woolen or cotton balls. He is believed to have lived in Massachusetts. The wooden frame is a product of an unknown craftsman. The screen kept drafts out of an unlit fireplace.

Art Nouveau Barset

Mixed material, 11½ x 19⅜;
France, 1905. A French artisan
with the initials ''E.H.''
designed and rendered this
hand-cut ''fretwork'' decanter.
Two crystal aperitif decanters
and eight glasses accompany the
piece.

"A La Recherche Du Contact"

Walter Thor. Stained-glass, 77 x 60; France, 1904. Thor painted the original art for this stained glass as part of his contract word for Kossuth Co. of Paris. Kossuth produced posters and billboards and marketed them throughout Europe. Granelly and Co. of Barcelona, Spain acquired the rights to Thor's image in 1906. This stained glass work, consisting of more than 200 pieces, is the largest known pre-1920 automotive stained glass window. Thor's original artwork is presented above.

Cloth Square

Cotton, 17⅝ x 17⅝; attributed to Switzerland, ca. 1904.

Lap Rugs

Textile, ca. 1905. Keeping warm in early automobiles was a problem partially solved through the use of lap rugs. The German rug *(top left)* was hand-dyed and portrays a male-oriented racing scene, while the French rug *(bottom left)* depicts the use of a child's lap rug, projecting an image of warmth, protection and family. Both items were produced around 1905.

"On Holiday"

Unsigned. Silk, 7¼ x 11⅞; Austria, 1905. Silks depicting a chauffeured couple speeding toward the coast for holiday were produced in various sizes for the Daimler Motor Car Company.

Untitled

Machine-woven cotton and silk,
19 x 19; England, ca. 1905.

Advertisement

Glass, 18 x 26; New York, ca. 1906. An advertising sign for the General Accident Automobile Insurance Company of Philadelphia, this embossed glass sign was made by the Rodier and Fitzgerald Glass Sign Company, Pearl St., New York City.

Salad Condiment Set

Crystal, 6 x 9¼; Europe, ca.
1906.

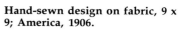

"You Auto Shave"

Hand-sewn design on fabric, 9 x
9; America, 1906.

Menu Marker

Silk, 5½ x 3¾; England, ca.
1906.

"Automobiles DeDion-Bouton"

François Danton. Tapestry, 40¾ x 64; France, 1906. During the reign of Louis XIV, the town of Aubusson, France was distinguished as the official tapestry producer for the King of France. Marquis DeDion, a founding member of the Automobile Club of France, recognized about the time of the Gordon Bennett Race in 1903 that he could market a limousine-style car throughout France. The Marquis presumably retained the skills of master weaver Danton, whose family had produced tapestry for generations, to design at least six of these wall tapestries for display in the DeDion-Bouton showrooms in major French cities. Danton brilliantly threaded tens of thousands of hand-dyed woolen and silken strings into this "low weave" carpet, a centuries-old style.

Rug

Textile, 35 x 60; America, ca. 1908. A small "scatter rug" attributed to American production, made of cotton thread with jute backing.

Victorian Lamp

Unsigned. Glass on metal base, 21 x 14; America, ca. 1907. A hand-painted glass lamp depicting an early racing scene on a dirt horsetrack. The scene incorporates race cars, an early Wright flyer, balloons and bicycles with a clubhouse and grandstand similar to that of the Empire Race Track, today known as Yonkers Racecourse.

Muffler bag

Eatiana. Silk, 11 x 6⅞; France, ca. 1909. This colorful silk muffler bag depicts a child and pussycat in a pedal car and was hand-painted by Eatiana in France.

Motor Car

Ivory, ½ x 8⅞; India, ca. 1915. Attributed to Indian origins, this hand-carved ivory object portrays a couple of British origin, judging by their dress, chauffeured by a man wearing Hindu garb.

Souvenir Dish

Glass, 2¾ x 5; England, 1909. *(left)* Made of molded glass, this auto-shaped object was made in England and given to "Lydia."

"Bremen Prize"

Unsigned. Marble, 11½ x 28½; Germany, 1919. *(right)* Awarded to Hermann Wittgenstein for a race held in Bremen, Germany in December.

"The Sparker"

Imprinted fabric, 20 x 20; America, ca. 1910. Pillow cover. *(above)*

"L'Transportation"

Attributed to Alfred-Jean Halou (1875-1939). Plaster, 21½ x 13¼; France, 1919. *(left)* This object was created and shown at the Paris Exhibition. Halou also produced statuary work that is represented at the Musée d'Art Moderne in Paris and the Musée de Blosi, the city of his birth.

"Auto Circuit"

Lafon Mollo. Plaster, 15 x 9½; France, 1909. *(right)* This delightful work depicts typical "tourists" of early motoring, with the man taking a photograph, while the woman draws the attention of the subject.

Lamp

Mixed media, 18½ x 9¼;
France, ca. 1925. A classic
representation of an automotive
subject lamp from the Art Deco
period, the hand-painted globe
features three sedans traveling
along a country road. The stem
and base are made of mirrored
glass. Originally, the lamp set
upon an octagonal-shaped base.

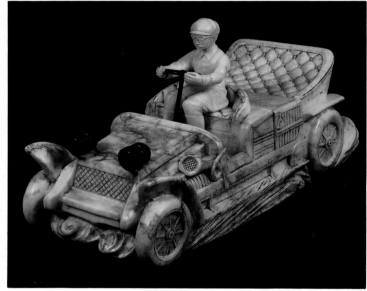

"L'Automobiliste"

Unsigned. Marble, 14 x 29½;
France, ca. 1920.

"Resta's Victory at Indianapolis"

A. Kow and Jilsk. Plaster, 16⅛ x 23; France, ca. 1922. This plaster commemorates the 1916 victory of Dario Resta at the Indianapolis Speedway. Resta won the 500-mile event on May 30, driving a Peugeot (number 17) at an average speed of 84.05 mph. Resta was the last winner at Indy before America's involvement in World War I. The 500-mile race would not start again until 1919.

Alexis Kow, one of the two artists who cooperated on the project, later produced automotive art work for the Peugeot company. He probably conceived the idea for the object from an illustration by T.M. Wilder in the May 29, 1913 issue of *Motor Age* magazine, which highlighted the Indianapolis race. Wilder portrayed a goddess with arms extended over the drivers and mechanics of three cubist style cars to highlight a racing poem written by J.C. Burton, titled "To America's Defenders."

Glass

Automotive glassware objects were popular and affordable in the early days of motoring. Clockwise from above left:

Aperitif decanter with hand-painted scene of motor car and woman flying an aeroplane, France, ca. 1910.

Crystal wine glass with serpentine stem and etched motoring image, France, ca. 1915.

Apertif decanter with etched racing scene, France, ca. 1909.

Glass mug with four men in an open touring car, with the legend ''Cheers to the Chauffeur,'' Germany, ca. 1925.

Scotch decanter with hand-painted scene of driver flying over wall after car crash, legend reads ''Car For Sale-Owner Taking To Air Travel,'' England, ca. 1909.

Aperitif decanter of blown glass with motoring scene, England, ca. 1900.

Liquor decanter in the shape of a tire, with the cork seal and lid manufactured in sterling silver, England, ca. 1919.

"Elizabeth Junek"

Antonio Giorgi. Marble, 15¾ x 15½; Italy, 1927. *(left)* As a child, Elizabeth Junek experienced the excitement and adventure brought to European society during the "Heroic Days" of motoring. To her, the automobile represented speed and mobility, as well as a challenge that could set her apart. Junek, protective of her private life, was very selective about her participation in races. In 1927, she became the first woman to compete in the coveted Targa-Florio Race, capturing the hearts of Italian men, who read of her "brave and heroic" deeds in the nation's newspapers. Giorgi sculpted this outstanding work in his studio near Polizzi, a small town on the Targa-Florio racing circuit.

"Male Racer"

Vito Gimto. Marble, 18¼ x 17⅜; Italy, ca. 1925. *(right)*

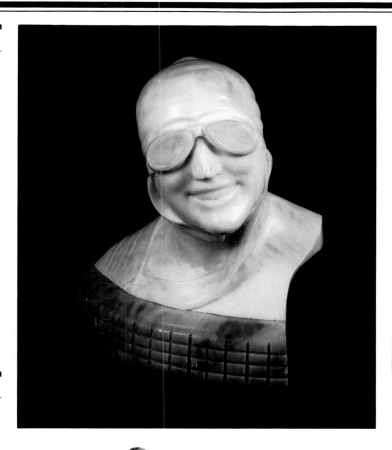

"Bugatti at San Sebastian"

Eduoard Diosi. Marble, 11½ x 29½; France, 1926. Diosi's recognition as an artist came in the early Twenties. In this work, he captures Jules Goux winning the Grand Prix d'Europe at San Sebastian in a Type 37 Bugatti. Goux also won the French Grand Prix that year and placed second in the Spanish Grand Prix.

"The Motorist"

Wood, 10½ x 4½; England, ca. 1930.

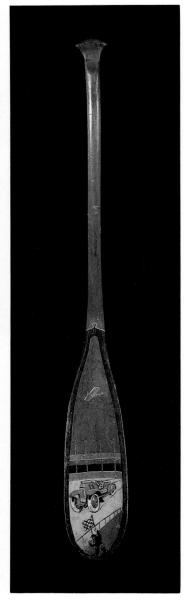

Oar

Wood, 15¾ x 6½; America, 1929. A folk artist painted this boat oar with a racing car passing a timing official as an airplane passes overhead. Various markings indicate the object was part of a fraternal organization in 1929.

"Lady Racer"

Attributed to Antonio Giorgi.
Marble, 14 x 10; Italy, ca. 1927.

5

PLAYTHINGS

TOYS HAVE BEEN a part of human life throughout the ages. All cultures of the world have toys. Made for and enjoyed by children, they are an integral part of youth that provides countless hours of enjoyment, learning and pleasure. The origin of toys are rooted in the culture of society for they are a miniaturization of mankind's history, pastimes, dreams and fulfillment. Throughout the centuries, toys have served as a stimulus, allowing the child the opportunity to imitate the experience of "being adult" or to learn the skills of survival. Primitive-age parents hand-fashioned toys from stone, tree branches or other natural materials found in the environment. Making a stick into a toy spear not only allowed a primitive child to pass time in simple play, it also taught the skills of stalking and hunting necessary for survival in a harsh and competitive environment. Such a stick over time has evolved into a baseball bat or hockey stick that today allows the child to enjoy playtime and be trained in the skills and ability that can lead to competition in the sports arena. Perhaps the joy stick of our television games will provide the basic skills for tomorrow's adult to handle the computerized age that is upon us.

The toys of children vary from simple to complex, based on the sophistication level of a given culture. The natural materials used for the toys of primitive children emerged into exploding toys such as rockets and flares in China of 5000 years ago, the movable-limb doll of Egypt 4000 years ago, the metal toy soldiers of Europe's Middle Ages, and the paper games and puzzles of America's eighteenth century. Wheels have been prominent on European toys since Greece in the first century B.C., but in the Americas, the wheel was not introduced until the arrival of the Conquistadors, thus creating a tremendous surprise for archaeologists when a primitive clay toy with wheels was found in pre-Columbian Mexican ruins.

The nineteenth century brought the Industrial Revolution and new methods of manufacturing toys. Basic principles of physical science, such as the swinging pendulum, weight counterbalancing, application of centrifugal force and magnetic fields were applied in the construction of toys. Toys, such as those made of tin beginning in the Eighteen-hundreds, were more often found in

"Coupe Gordon Bennet"

S. Gunthermann. Lithograph tin, 5⅝ x 11⅞; Germany, 1903. This toy was inspired by the body design of the new Mors vehicles entered in Gordon Bennett race. The shamrock on the hood indicates that the race was held at Ballyshannon, Ireland, on July 2, 1903.

the nurseries of children of wealth and royalty. By the time of the Victorian Age, such toys would be created in mass numbers for children of all classes through the development of the machine press. They were then decorated by chromolithography before the metal sheet was formed, or by hand-enamelling after the parts were assembled. Sometimes a combination of both was used to complete the final product.

As the "horseless carriage" came of age in the mid-Eighteen-hundreds, toys imitating its development were initially made by local toymakers, whittlers and folkcrafters to please the child. By 1895, particularly after newsmaking races in Europe such as the Paris-Bordeaux-Paris Race and America's Chicago-Evanston Race, larger toy manufacturers began to recognize what automobilists already knew, that with time the motor car would become a major influence on society. Exploiting the potential of the automotive-styled toy in the marketplace, some manufacturers such as those in the tin toy industry, began to retool for the projected demand. Excellent examples of such "transition" period toys are seen in the Gunthermann toys. American manufacturers such as Ives, Stevens, Wilkins, Weeden and others continued to improve the quality of toys constructed from mixed materials and cast iron after the turn of the century. A greater sophistication in toy quality, design and production was noticeable in products shown in toy catalogues around 1903 and 1904. The continued success of the Gordon Bennett Races resulted in the production of many automotive toy lines with mechanisms by German companies such as Bing, Carette, and Marklin and French firms such as Fernand Martin, Jep, and Charles Rossignol.

The art in creating, designing and developing toys of the early automotive period was extended to many other areas of toy manufacturing. French pedal cars gained popularity around 1906, while an outstanding reed automotive-styled baby carriage line was being produced in America by the Haywood-Wakefield Company in 1908. Countless tin butterfly boxes, holiday ornaments, papier-maché candy containers and a wide variety of other toy products emerged during the period.

The toy, in one form or another, shall be the plaything of children of all ages forever. The mechanical automotive toy of yesteryear gave way to the plastic battery-operated toy of the present, while the emergence of the computerized light beam activated toy sets is on the horizon of children's play.

"Country Ride" Puzzle

McLaughlin Brothers.
Lithograph cardboard, 9 x 16;
America, ca. 1900. *(above)*

Animated Motor Car Pulltoy

Mixed Media, 8¼ x 10⅜;
France, ca. 1898. This
delightful, well-designed toy is
highlighted by a hand-woven
wicker back support, pressed-
tin body, wire wheels and a
papier maché animal driver. As
the toy is pulled, the right arm
of the animal goes up and
down, ringing the small bell
attached to its hand. Of Art
Nouveau styling, the toy is
attributed to French origins
from the late Eighteen-nineties.

Jester Motor Car Pulltoy

Wood, 10½ x 8½; France, ca.
1898. *(left)* An ornate wooden
toy of a child wearing a jester
suit with arms that move up
and down, as he sits in a car.

"Curved Dash Olds"

Acme Manufacturing Company. Steel, 7 x 10⅜; America, 1904. Inspired by the Ransom E. Olds' "Curved Dash Olds," this toy was made from pressed steel. Olds' motor car was the first full-sized, mass-produced vehicle made in the United States. Olds sold 650 units in 1900 and the car gained steady popularity with the general public. It also inspired period songs such as Gus Edwards' "In My Merry Oldsmobile," written in 1905.

Merry-Go-Round

Mixed media, 21¾ h.; France, ca. 1903. This French musical merry-go-round was made by an unknown French manufacturer after the Gordon Bennett Race in Ireland in 1903. The quaint and colorful toy has a clockwork music box and it delights children with its appearance, motion and sound. The lithograph tin cars, attributed to Georges Carette of Germany, are attached by hand and had dolls in the seats. Four of these toys are known to exist.

Panhard Toy

S. Gunthermann. Lithograph
tin, 5⅝ x 11; Germany, 1903.
The Panhard racer was in
production from 1903 through
1909, by which time many toys
were reflecting body styles of
the A.C.F.'s Grand Prix.

"Electric Runabout"

Clark Manufacturing Co. Wood,
steel and cast iron, 6¼ x 7;
America, ca. 1900.

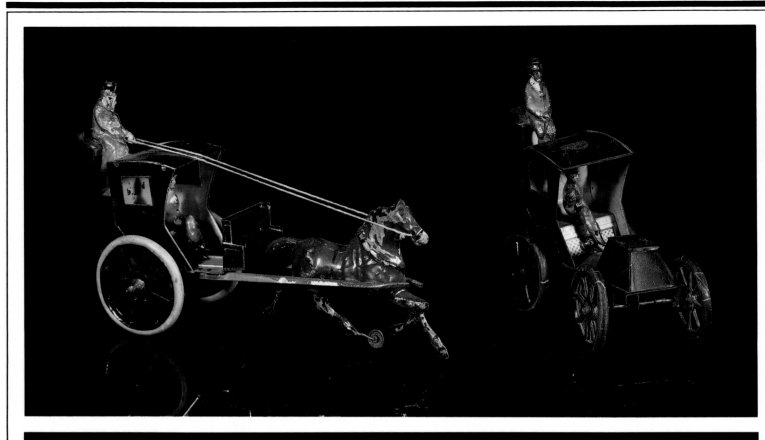

Transitional Auto

Ives Manufacturing Company. Cast iron, 6 x 7¼; America, ca. 1899.

Transition Toys

S. Gunthermann. Top: Lithograph tin; left: 5⅜ x 8½; right: 5⅜ x 5½. The horse-drawn hansom cab gave way to the motor driven automobile of a later age. Such toys are called "transition toys" because the carriage body style basically remained the same, but the horse was replaced with the motor bonnet, representing the transition in mobility at the time.

Bottom: Lithograph tin; left: 5 x 6⅛; right: 5 x 11¼. The other example of "transition toys" were of French production about the same era as the Gunthermann line, from 1904 to 1912. Inventories of such lines were still offered for sale in catalogues as late as 1914. All of the toys are lithograph tin and are clockwork driven. The French toys have a mechanism which apparently was manufactured in Germany, exported to France and installed on this particular piece. The installation of parts such as wheels, mechanisms, steering wheels, and side lamps were oftentimes manufactured by one company and sold elsewhere. This common practice makes it exceptionally difficult to determine toy manufacturers who did not use identification marks or symbols.

TRANSITION TOYS

Transitional Auto

Ives Manufacturing Company.
Cast iron, 6¾ x 7¼; America,
ca. 1900.

Racing Set

Tin, 7 x 10; Bavaria, ca. 1903.
The cars were inspired by a
British Napier driven by S.F.
Edge, who won the Gordon
Bennett Race of 1902. The toy is
made of tin and is marked
"Ges. Gesch" which signifies a
pending patent on the product.

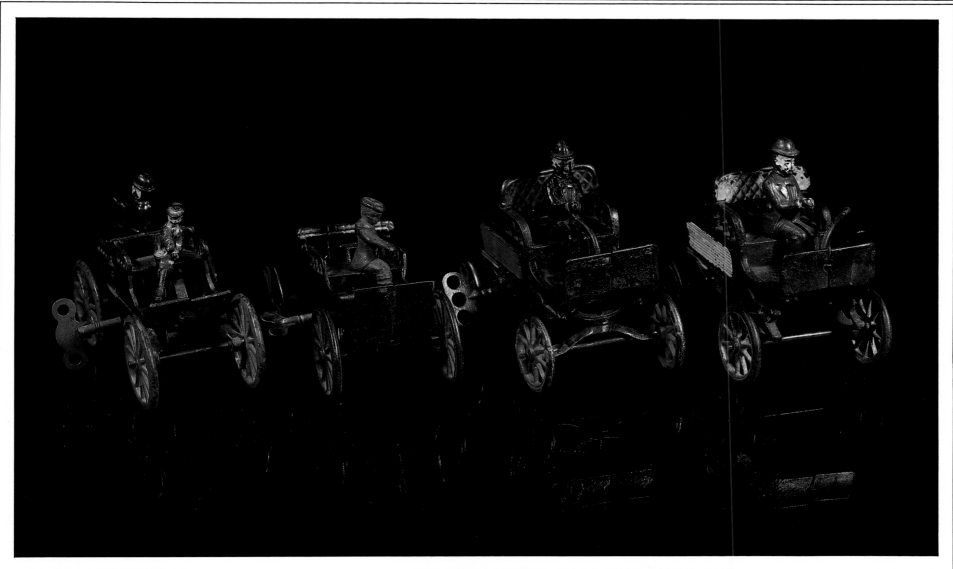

Cast Iron Toys

Range in size 4⅛ x 5⅞ to 5¾ x 7¼; America. Left to right:

"Motor Hunting Trap" by the Edward R. Ives Company, ca. 1895. This piece has a clockwork mechanism.

"Motor Buckboard" attributed to Stevens and Brown Manufacturing Company, ca. 1898. Has a clockwork mechanism.

"Runabout" by Ives, ca. 1898. has a clockwork mechanism.

"Runabout" by Harris manufacturing Company, ca. 1901.

Happy Nak Tea Set

Tin, 6⅝ x 9⅝; Great Britain, ca. 1904. *(left)* Children's tin tea play sets were highly popular in the early Teens. This tin tray is part of the "Happy Nak" series produced in Great Britain with "Tabby & Company" and "Terrier & Company" serving as proprietors of the confectionery and tobacco shops respectively.

Puzzle

Lithograph paper on wood, 15¼ x 11⅜; France, ca. 1903. A six-sided puzzle made by J.L. of Paris allowed the child to change scenes by turning the puzzle blocks. This colorful toy was made of lithograph paper on wood and sold in a sturdy, wooden box.

"The Auto Race" Puzzle

Lithograph on cardboard, 10 x 15; America, ca. 1904. This puzzle was distributed as an advertising toy for the C.I. Hood Sasparilla Company of Lowell, Massachusetts.

Egg shaped containers

Mixed media, range in size 2 x 4¾ to 2⅞ x 7⅛; Germany, 1903-1915. All of these pieces are made of cardboard and papier maché except the smallest, which is made of tin. These egg-shaped containers with automotive images stirred the imagination of children with their chickens, rabbits and peers driving. Even more enjoyable was the reward found inside.

Tea Set

Lithograph tin, (tray) 8¼ x 11 (cups) 2 to 4¼ h.; Germany. Children's lithograph tin tea sets with automotive, nautical and aeronautical images were mass-produced in Germany and exported to other European countries in the years before World War I.

Mechanical Toys

Left: "Bonnet Phaeton" Wilkins Toy Company. Pressed steel and cast iron, 5⅛ x 9; America, 1905.

Right: "Phaeton" Wilkins Toy Company. Pressed steel and cast iron, 5⅛ x 9; America, ca. 1902. Both have clockwork mechanisms.

Wooden Toys

Below, left: Wood, 4½ x 6⅜; France, ca. 1906. Cabriolet "bon-bon" container exquisitely fabricated with silk cloth over cardboard.

Below, right: Wood, 6⅛ x 5¾; America, ca. 1903. Wooden pull toy with cloth covered figurine.

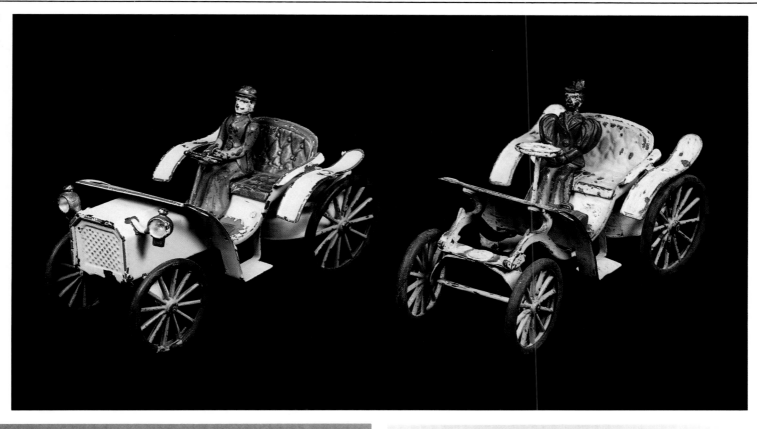

"Steam Automobile"

Weeden Manufacturing of Connecticut. Painted tin, 5¼ x 8½; America, ca. 1902. *(above)*

Production years for this toy were from 1900 to 1903. The toy was given to children as a premium for selling ten subscriptions of *American Youth Companion* magazine.

221

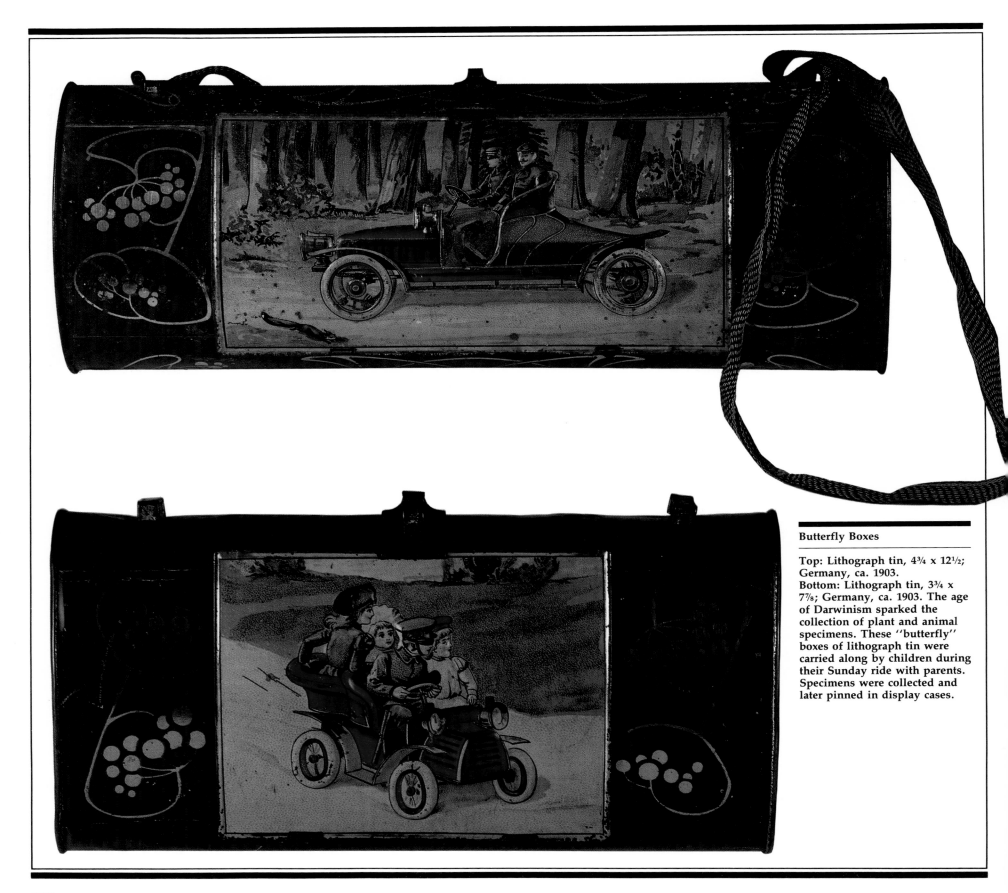

Butterfly Boxes

Top: Lithograph tin, 4¾ x 12½; Germany, ca. 1903.
Bottom: Lithograph tin, 3¾ x 7⅞; Germany, ca. 1903. The age of Darwinism sparked the collection of plant and animal specimens. These "butterfly" boxes of lithograph tin were carried along by children during their Sunday ride with parents. Specimens were collected and later pinned in display cases.

"Nippon Diorama Story Box"

Unsigned. Paper, glass and wood, 3 x 4⅝; Japan, 1840 to 1910. This rare and unique toy allowed the child to crank and visualize 12 scenes portraying prominent events in transportation, culture and trade that occurred in Japan from 1840 to 1910.

"Horseless Carriage"

Kenton Manufacturing
Company. Cast iron, 5⅞ x 7⅜;
ca. 1902. Toy is powered by a
clockwork mechanism.

"Single Seaters"

S. Gunthermann. Lithograph tin; Germany, ca. 1904. Left: 4½ x 6¼; right: 5¼ x 6⅜; Both have clockwork mechanism. Inspired by the Paris-Berlin Race of 1901, these toys depict the Mors race car driven by Fournier, winner of the race.

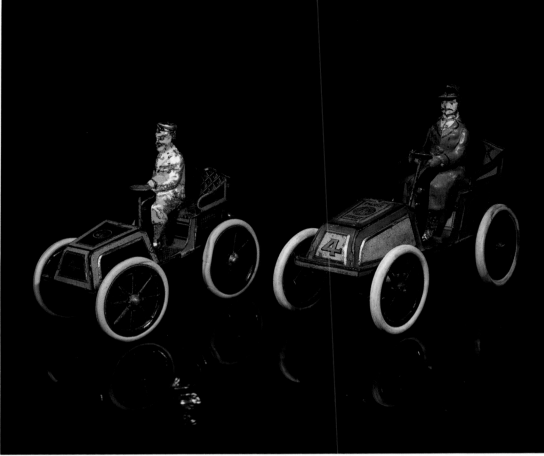

Tonneau Toy

Metal, 5 x 11⅞; America, ca. 1903. *(above)* This rear-entry tonneau by an unknown American manufacturer sports a forward and reverse gear, workable tiller steering wheel, sheet metal body, cast iron wheels and clockwork mechanism.

"Auto Racer" Toys

Wilkins. Pressed steel, left to right: 4 x 9¾, 3 x 7½, 4 x 9¾. Produced from 1902 to 1905 in various sizes and colors. The toy is powered by a clockwork mechanism.

"Motor Ride"

J.W. Spear & Sons. Cardboard with metal cars, 11⅜ x 16¼; England, date unknown. *(above)* This "jolly" board game was designed by the J.W. Spear & Sons Company of London and printed by a Spear factory in Bavaria. The game took the players on a motoring tour of the English countryside.

"Dollies Up To Date"

Misch & Company. Paper and cardboard, 12¾ x 9¼; England, ca. 1907. *(right)* Printed in Germany, Misch marketed this product in England, America, France and Germany.

"Plinker"

Tin, 6⅝ x 3⅛; Germany, ca. 1907. *(left)* German-made "plinker" tin toys such as this one for the French marketplace became highly popular with the growth of amusement parks and fairgrounds throughout Europe.

''The Breakdown''

Walter Appleton Clark.
Lithograph cardboard, 11 x 8;
America, 1905. Clark produced
this image the year before he
died. F. Collier & Sons created
and distributed it as a
children's puzzle in 1908.

"Runabout Autos"

Left: Fallows Company. Painted tin, 6⅝ x 5¼; America, ca. 1895.

Middle: Fallows Company. Tin, 6⅞ x 5⅜; America, ca. 1897. A string-operated spool "motor" provided the source of energy for this toy. The paper label on the base, "Patent August 16, 1898," is the date Fallows received the patent to press artistic images on tin.

Right: Arcade Manufacturing Co. Mixed media, 5 x 8⅞; America, ca. 1908. Lillian Gottschalk, in her book, *American Toy Cars & Trucks*, states that this toy was possibly the "first automobile produced by Arcade."

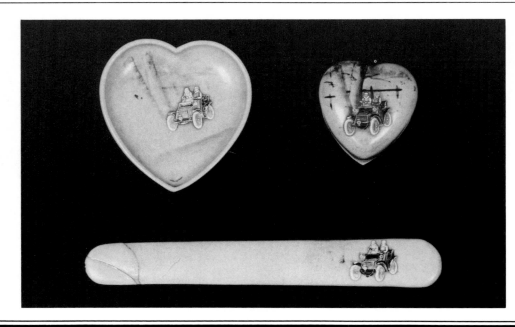

Child's Desk Set

Celluloid, 2-7 d.; France, ca. 1907. *(left)* These were given to children for buttons, trinkets and opening letters.

Games and Toys

Hand-held toys were often purchased for children to occupy their time on tour or during motoring picnics and events. All of the following have an automotive image on the face of the object.

Top row, left: Hand cranked music box, Germany, 1910.

Top row, right: ''Plinker'' toy with candy compartment, Germany, ca. 1908.

Middle row, three objects at left: Marble games made in Germany from 1908 to 1910.

Middle row, right: ''Auto Watch'' with movable hands and race cars, Germany, ca. 1910.

Bottom row, left three: All marble games from Germany.

Bottom row, right: ''Mercedes SS'' marble game, Germany, 1928.

"Motoring Tin Toys"

S. Gunthermann. Lithograph tin. Both toys are clockwork driven.

Above: 6¾ x 10⅛; 1905. This four-passenger touring car was popular with children around 1905. It carries a license plate number J.B.242 and has a body style similar to an early Mors or Clement-Bayard.

Opposite: 7⅛ x 8¼; ca. 1903. This toy was inspired by an early Daimler automobile and reflects the affluent couple being chauffeured on their tour.

Tea set

Ceramic, (tea set) 1½-7½ high and 2½-7½ wide; cereal bowls 5⅛-7⅝ d. A large variety of children's tea sets, cereal bowls, piggy banks and other playthings were manufactured with automotive images over the years.

Opposite, above and below left: A tea set by Orla Porcelain Company. Germany, ca. 1908.

Opposite, below right: A selection of dishes produced by Grindley Banquet Ware Company of England, the Unity and Altenberg Porcelain companies of Germany and Nipponware by Noritake, Japan. All of these dishes are ca. 1906.

Right: A tea set with matching "barrel" bank and candy cap dish manufactured by Altenburg China Company. Germany, ca. 1905.

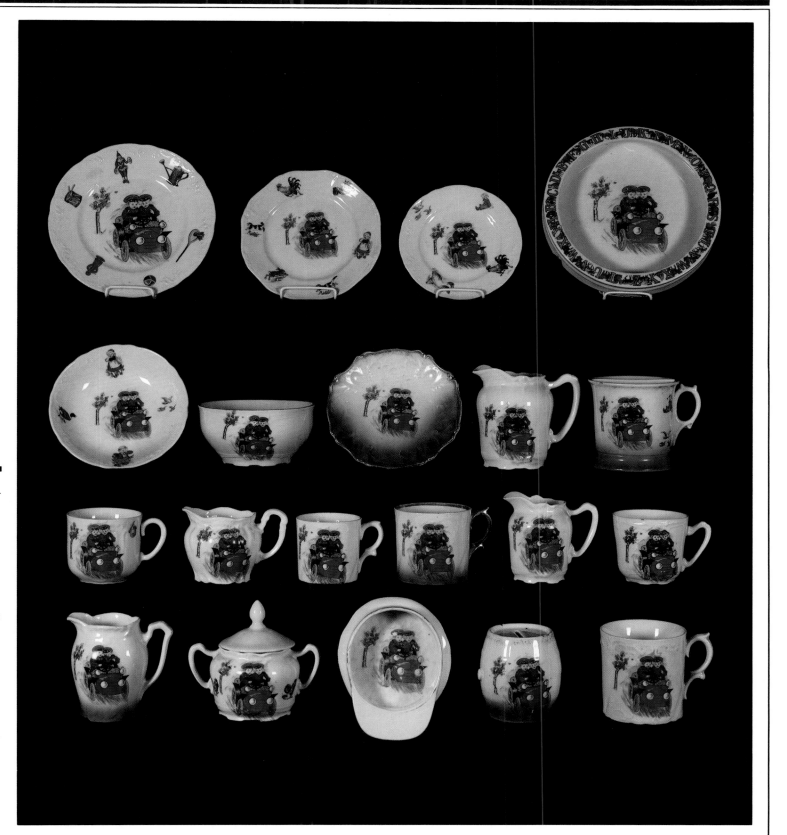

Baby Carriage

Wood and metal, 28¼ x 36½;
European, ca. 1916.

Baby Carriage

Heywood-Wakefield Company.
Wicker, 38 x 46½; America, ca.
1908. This rare baby carriage
was designed and manufactured
by the Heywood-Wakefield
company in the United States.
Its body is made entirely of
handwoven reed or "wicker,"
with the compartment totally
lined in cloth. The roof is
detachable for warm weather,
while the windscreen or foul-
weather curtain serves to protect
the infant during brisk fall and
winter days. The wheels are
detachable allowing a pair of
sleigh runners to be attached for
use on snow or ice. A rear-axle
foot brake secures the carriage
from coasting. The front license
plate is numbered "H.W.492
W" and the original ad reads
"in beauty of design, quality
and workmanship, in special
features for baby's comfort, no
line equals the Heywood-
Wakefield."

STANDARD OIL CO. OF N.J.
STANDARD MOTOR OIL
STANDARD
STANDARD
348
S
M

Esso Service Station

Lithograph tin, 12⅝ x 19 x 31⅝ deep; Germany, ca. 1921. The station, with lubrication pump wagons and service lift produced by Doll & Cie., features a Kingsberry tow truck from the same era.

"Auto Garage"

Muller and Kadeder. Lithograph tin, 7⅜ x 11¾; Germany, ca. 1912.

"Silent Movie Car"

Nifty Company. Lithograph tin, 4⅜ x 9¾; Germany, ca. 1913. Powered by clockwork mechanism, the cameraman turns the handle of the camera as the car moves forward.

"Auto Polo"

Tellus Company. Lithograph tin, 4⅛ x 6¾; Germany, ca. 1912. This toy is powered by a clockwork mechanism that moves the car forward when the polo player swings his stick. Auto polo was a competitive team game played at fairgrounds in Europe and the United States from 1909 through 1914. Due to numerous fatalities and disabilities, the game was banned in America in 1925. A painting by O. Reynolds on page 45 presents the game in action being played on a New York fairground in 1913.

"Confrontation Car"

Hans Eberl. Lithograph tin, 4⅜ x 11⅛; Germany, ca. 1912. This car is powered by a clockwork mechanism. The animal strikes the car's radiator when in motion. Eberl incorporated the "Jester" image found on this novelty toy after 1906.

"Famous Lionel Racing Electric Automobiles"

Lionel Company. Metal, 4 x 8; America, ca. 1915. The toy is the first known electric automotive racing set.

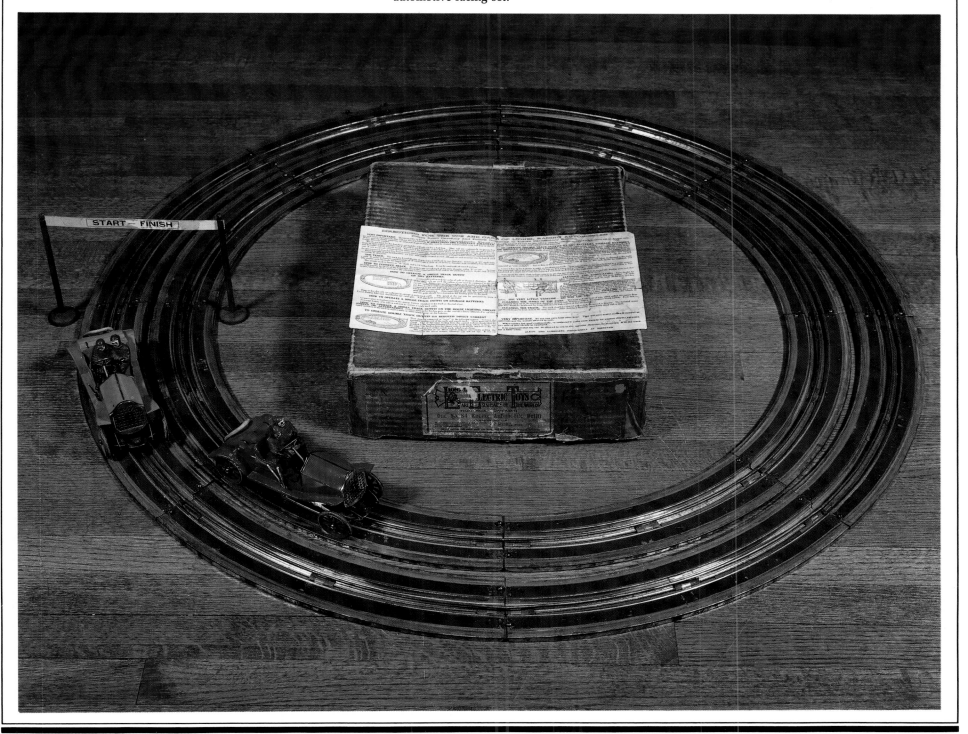

''Jeu des Tourists''

Saussine of Paris. Game board with metal cars and die, 13¼ x 14¾; France, 1919. This delightful and educational game board allowed the players to ''tour'' through France learning about cities, geography, history and products made in different regions. Flat metal cars marked the progress of the player after the roll of die.

''Automobile Amphibian Car''

Attributed to S. Gunthermann. Tin with spring-drive, 4 x 7¾; Germany, ca. 1910.

Paper Cardboard Toys

Top and center: Both vehicles are made of lithograph paper on cardboard and were produced by the Illustrated Lithograph Company of New York between 1919 and 1930.

Bottom row: A selection of wood and paper mint containers produced in the United States, ca. 1908-1913.

''Froggie the Chauffeur''

Papier maché, 7⅜ x 7¼; Germany, ca. 1919.

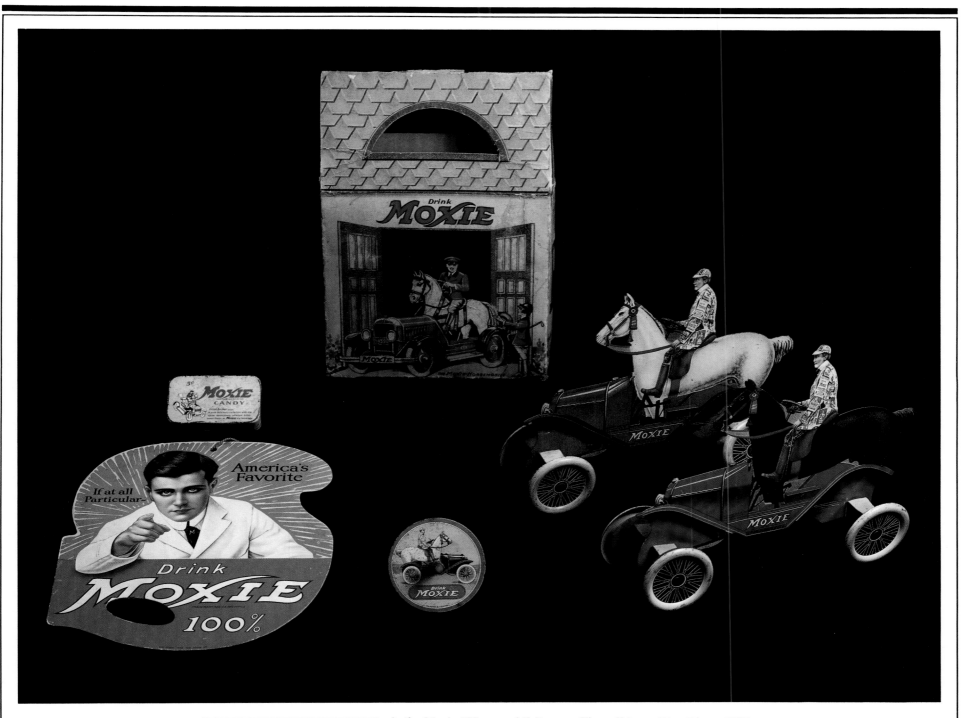

Moxie Toys

Moxie Cola was a popular American soft drink produced in the United States as early as 1916. In 1917, Frank M. Archer, the genius behind the drink, began a marketing campaign for his product. Most remembered is the Moxie "Horsemobile" which became the stalwart of the campaign, as shown on the lithograph tin on page 94 and the toys shown above. Clockwise from top:

Moxie Cola carrier with the Horsemobile image, 10 x 6¾; America, ca. 1929.

Tin pull toys, 6¾ x 8½; ca. 1917.

Toy top with lithograph by Charles W. Showk Company, 2½ deep; 1918.

Child's fan, 8 x 7; 1918.

A Moxie five cent candy tin, 1⅝ x 2¾; America, ca. 1925.

Candy containers

Papier maché, *(Far left)* 4¾ x 3⅜ and *(left)* 3⅜ x 4; Germany, ca. 1920. These candy containers were produced by confectioners to be sold to children for special events or holidays. The chauffeur container carried sweets during a tour, while the jack-o-lantern may have been filled with bon-bons on All Saint's Day. Other popular containers of the period were Santa Claus and the Easter Rabbit. Oftentimes and in the case of the two objects shown here, the containers would be converted into lanterns after the goodies were finished. A simple candle would bring the eyes, nose and mouth alive as it glowed in the dark.

Sweets Container

Lithograph tin, 4⅜ x 6½; France, ca. 1923. *(below)* Huntley and Palmer, Ltd. initiated the marketing of cookies and biscuits in novelty tins in the early Eighteen-nineties. Such novel ideas were continued into the late Twenties, particularly by English firms. This "sweet car" lithograph tin container was manufactured in France for use with candy and cookies.

"The Auto Harmonica"

M. Hohner. 1¾ x 5; Germany, 1924. This harmonica has fourteen notes and a 1½ octave mouthpiece.

"Auto Build 5 in 1 Toy"

A. Schoenhut Company. Wood and tin, 4½ x 11¼; America, 1925. This creative design allowed the child to construct either a racer, roadster, coupe, limousine or delivery wagon from the parts, which were all interchangeable and could be taken apart for re-use.

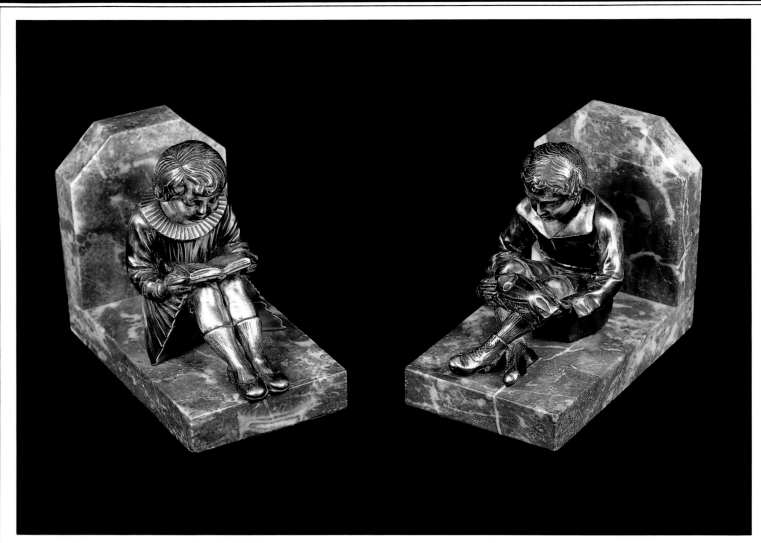

4½ x 5⅛; France, ca. 1924. A pair of bookends feature a young girl reading a book and a boy looking at a race car.

Candy Molds

Children have always loved candy and by 1908, German confectioners were able to use metal alloy molds to image the automobile in chocolate. The confectionery practice spread to France, then throughout Europe and America, quickly allowing children to eat all models, all years whenever mom and dad were, or were not, looking. Range: 1¾-4¾ x 6⅝-7½. Clockwise from upper left:

''Auto Rabbit'' LeTance Company, France, 1910.

''Open Tourer'' manufactured for Von Emden Candy Company in New York by an unknown German maker, ca. 1925.

''Sedan'' manufactured for Von Emden of New York by a German maker, ca. 1925.

''Horseless Carriage'' Germany, ca. 1908.

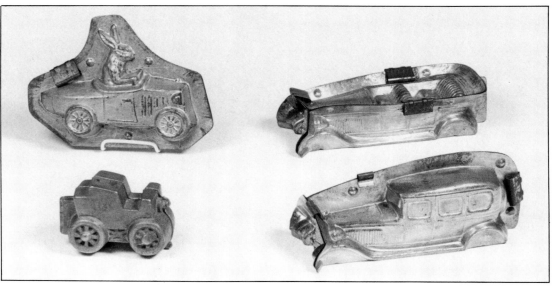

Schuco Toys

Left: "Monkey Car" Schuco Toy Company. Sheet metal with cloth, 6⅝ x 6⅛; Germany, ca. 1926. As the string is pulled, the monkey moves its left arm and mouth while producing a "squeaking" sound.

Right: "Wunder Auto" Schuco Toy Company. Sheet metal with cloth, 5 x 7⅜; Germany, ca. 1925. Powered by a clockwork mechanism.

Hubley Toys

Left to right: Cast iron, 4¼ x 9¾, 5¼ x 11¾, 6 x 9¾; America, 1925-1935. The Hubley Manufacturing Company of Lancaster, Pennsylvania produced most of its automotive toys from the mid-Twenties through the early Thirties. The open touring car on the left has the same bodystyle as the roofed vehicle on the right. A "Say It With Flowers" Indian motorcycle manufactured in 1929 was popular then and still is very desirable among collectors today. All of these toys are made of cast iron, a practice Hubley abandoned in 1942 due to commitment to fulfill war contracts.

Child's Car

Mixed media, 29½ x 43; France, ca. 1905. This one-seat sprocket-drive pedal car was inspired by the Panhard Motor Car and produced in France. The side lamps were produced by Joseph Lucas, Ltd. of Birmingham, England. Many full-size European head lamps and side lamps were also manufactured by this reputable English firm.

Child's Car

Mixed media, 28 x 72; France, ca. 1906. An exemplary two-seat pedal car with sprocket drive, given to a certain young lady named Miss Madeleine Lecoevire Wallers, as a childhood gift.

Pedal Car

''Fairey Auto-Coaster''
Worthington Company of Ohio,
Mixed media; 23 x 38; America,
1909. *(above left)*

Pedal Car

''149'' Mixed media, 28 x 56¾;
France, ca. 1910. *(above right)*

Pedal Car

''Packard Deluxe'' Gendron
Wheel Company. Mixed media,
29½ x 65½; America, 1923. *(left)*

Child's Car

Mixed media, 39⅜ x 57¾; France, ca. 1909. A charming single-seat pedal car with storage area under the hood and seat. A spark arrestor and gear control rod are found on the steering wheel, with compression control rod levers and a benzine primer pump on the dashboard. A gear lever and working hand brake are levered to the right of the driver. The craftsmanship in this toy is outstanding, even incorporating a child's tool kit under the seat. The pedal car is believed to be one of a kind, probably made for a fortunate child in a shop of a family associated with the manufacture of full-size motorcars.

Pedal Car

"Jordan" Murray Products Company. Mixed media, 28½ x 53; America, ca. 1927.

Pedal Car

Murray Ohio Manufacturing Company. Steel, rubber and leather, 23 x 53½; America, ca. 1936. This sleek, classic-bodied pedal car with inflatable Goodyear Tires was produced by the Murray Ohio Manufacturing Company in Cleveland, Ohio and sold under the trade name "Steelcraft."

Pedal Car

''Packard Tourer'' American
National Company. Mixed
media, 39 x 66½; America, ca.
1924.

Pedal Car

''Tourisimo'' Telas Moto-
Industria Argentina. Metal,
rubber and leather, 24 x 72¼;
Argentina, ca. 1929.

Pedal Car

''Roadster'' Mixed media, 27½
x 64⅜; European, ca. 1937. The
body is similar in design to
work by Fagoni and Falaschi.

PANHARD & LEVASSOR — 19 — Avenue d'Ivry — PARIS.

DAILY LIFE

THE AUTOMOBILE brought a new excitement to the masses who were curious about its purpose and function at the century's turn. Like the space shuttle or computer of the present, the motor car aroused interest and inquiry. For the most part, the common family would not be able to afford the purchase of a vehicle until mass production came of age ten years into the century. By this time the motoring industry, both in Europe and the United States, recognized that the female of the family had as much as "sixty percent of the influence in determining which marque would be purchased" for the household and addressed their marketing techniques accordingly.

Initially, souvenir concessionaires lead the way for inexpensive objects to be sold to the crowds attending motoring events. This was followed by motor car companies giving token gifts to potential purchasers (particularly women), motoring parts companies giving gifts to clients, and small shops producing motor car images on objects to be bought for the home. More expensive objects were to be found in specialty jewelry and craft shops, which produced artistic products for select audiences.

Such items were utilitarian in nature, incorporating the automobile's image on an object that could be handled or seen, or having some type of usefulness in daily life. Having such objects allowed motoring enthusiasts to feel they were part of an international movement drawing on this new form of mobility.

The artisan who produced the images on the inexpensive utilitarian items was usually employed in a company, unlike the commissioned artist who was retained by automobile clubs or motoring companies to produce fine art works such as paintings or sculpture. These company artists usually saw an automobile or image of an automobile in a magazine or newspaper and would then design the image or relief that went into the manufacturing process. Their designs were also limited by the company's desire to mass produce the product at low costs and greatest profits. Materials used in production were inexpensive and readily available, such as the metal alloys found in motoring style picture frames, ashtrays, coat buttons, souvenir spoons and pocketknives, cut glass or semi-precious stones used in the brooches, pins, cufflinks and other jewelry adornments; and celluloid for

Match Safes and Lighters

An exemplary selection of accessories with automotive or product images. Such items were attractive status symbols that also had practical use in lighting cigarettes or the carbide headlamps on the motor car for night driving. Sizes range 1³/₈ to 4¹/₄ x 1¹/₈ to 6¹/₈.

cigarette containers, hair brushes, combs and letter openers.

More intensive labor was necessary to manufacture items which took a combination of materials such as games and puzzles, pocket coin purses, the "mother of pearl" pin cushions and ink wells, celluloid photography books, with or without music boxes, and sewing/manicure sets.

The well-to-do motorist sought comparatively more expensive and "good taste" items which were purchased in fine jewelry shops. Objects used for utilitarian function were usually made of higher quality metals, the most favored being silver. Glove and cigar boxes made in England are superb examples of craftsmanship in this metal, many of which are highlighted with colored lithograph images created by Gilbert Wright, noted English landscape artist of the time.

The clocks and timepieces of the period varied in material usage as well as price. A high-quality clock of white metal made by Emile Bruchon or one of mixed metals commissioned by the Majarisha of Indore in the shape of a French limousine commanded a greater value than the more inexperienced work of Joelin with its lesser quality casting and post-pouring repairs. Similarly, handsomely crafted pocket watches that were popular with automobilists and produced by companies such as Perfection Watch Company and Systems Roskops oftentimes used quality Swiss movements made by outstanding firms such as A. Reymond of Zurich.

Tobacco smoking was a favorite pastime associated with motoring. Products such as match safes and containers to hold cigarettes, cigars and pipes soon found their way into the home, the auto club and the showroom. Most smoking paraphernalia was easy to produce out of inexpensive metal alloys, wood and celluloid. For more elegant gifts, the customer might have the jeweler create a specially designed sterling silver case, with a local artist retained to paint the favorite motoring car of the friend receiving the gift on the case's face.

In total, the automobile served as the theme for the production of millions of small and large objects that could be used in the home, at the office or motor club, in socialization, on tours or as remembrances. The utilitarian function of all of these objects allowed the motor car to be used, seen and desired in life on a day-to-day basis and certainly contributed to the overall romance, excitement and growth of the industry.

Horseless Carriage

Wood and copper, 7⅝ x 10⅞; France, 1898. *(top left)* A salesman's model of the Panhard-Levassor ''horseless carriage.''

Highway Locomotive

Mixed media, 7⅜ x 15; America, ca. 1860. *(top right)* A patent model constructed by the Robei company of Lincoln, Massachusetts as part of an attempt to obtain rights to produce its ''Highway Locomotive.''

Steam Stagecoach

Mixed media, 8¼ x 18½; America, ca. 1855. A patent model steam stagecoach.

PATENT MODELS

Perpetual Motion Model

Metal, 7¼ x 13⅝; America, ca. 1870. A hand-built model representing experimentation conducted on the concept of the ''perpetual motion wheel'' in the late eighteenth and early nineteenth centuries. The original device was designed, built and utilized by E.A. Tilly around 1810. An obscure American artist by the name of Gilbert illustrated this device in *Harper's Weekly* during the Eighteen-seventies using the wood engraving process. Gilbert was one of about 400 wood engravers in the United States at the time, a number that had swelled from only 20 three decades earlier. To this day, the concept has consumed a great deal of research energy but remains impractical under the laws of gravity.

Steam Carriage

Mixed media, 5¼ x 16¼; America, ca. 1850. A patent model of a multiple passenger steam carriage: the full-size operational vehicle, similar to this design, was in use on a regularly scheduled run in Philadelphia as early as 1854.

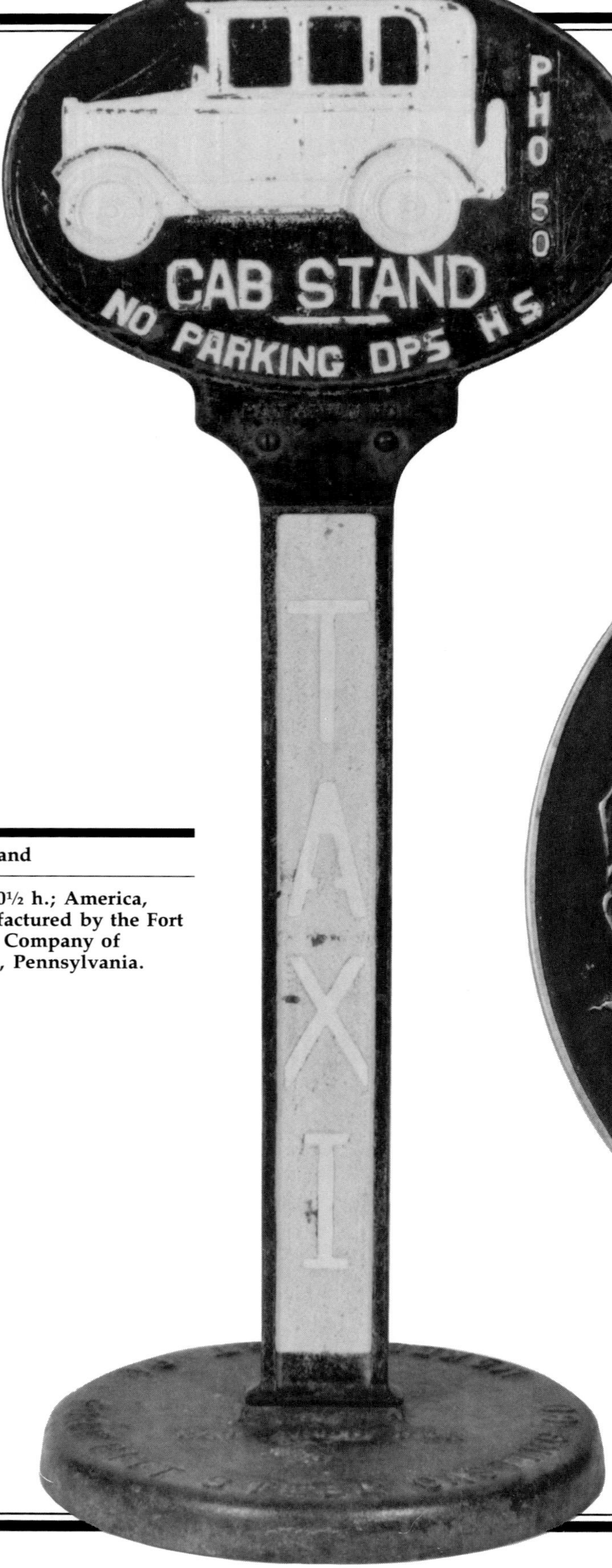

Taxi Cab Stand

Cast iron, 50½ h.; America, 1923. Manufactured by the Fort Pitt Casting Company of McKeesport, Pennsylvania.

Commemorative Plate

Aluminum, 10¾ d.; Germany, ca. 1933. A Mercedes commemorative plate made of aluminum and highlighting six vehicles, beginning with Karl Benz's tricycle through a 1930 coupe.

"Pastilles Valda"

Tin and wood, 18¾ x 32⅜; France, 1907. A descriptive pharmaceutical advertising sign promoting a lozenge product sold by Pastivel et Cie to motorists who suffered touring-related ailments such as "laryngitis, bronchitis, rheumatism, cataracts, influenza and lack of energy." The piece has a wind-up clockwork mechanism which activates movement in the doctor's right arm and in the wheels of the automobile.

Promotional Items

Many objects made of mixed materials were used to promote product lines for vehicle or personal use. Size range: 3⅛ to 5⅛ x 1¾ to 6⅜.

Top, left to right:
A tire pressure tester in a lithograph tin container. Michelin and Company, Clermont-Ferrand, France, ca. 1912.

E-Z Shoe Polish. Martin and Martin Company, Chicago, Illinois, ca. 1928.

A lithograph premium cup. Joplin (JOCO) Oil Company, America. Lithograph tin, ca. 1912.

Bottom, left to right:
Container box used to promote some unknown product of the "Williams' Suit Case for Men." America, cardboard, ca. 1917.

"Auto Suspensory." A cloth athletic supporter for male motorists produced by Bauer & Black. America, 1902.

"Traumaplast-Vervbande." A small first-aid kit for motoring mishaps. Germany, 1925.

Cigar Tins

Sizes range 2¾ to 5⅝ x 3 to 4⅛.

Left: Cigar tin containing 12 cigars for 5 cents. America, 1923.

Middle: Wall-mounted match holder. Gift of Gurlph Motor Car Company. Lithograph tin; Canada, ca. 1915.

Right: "Taxi Crimp Cut Tobacco" container. Imperial Company. Lithograph tin; Canada, ca. 1908.

Chocolate Tins

Items range in size 1½ to 4 x 2⅝ to 8½. (opposite)

Top: "Lloyd's Chocolates." Sold by Auerbach Candies of New York, 1920.

Bottom, left: "Auto-Laks Chocolates" provided "a pleasant and easy physic" on long tours. Crystal Chemical Company, New York, ca. 1921.

Bottom, middle: Candy container, Rowntree Cocoa Works, Ltd. Lithograph tin; England, ca. 1905.

Bottom, right: "Half Penny Savings Bank" for small members of the Driver's Chocolate Club. Lithograph tin; England, ca. 1908-1910.

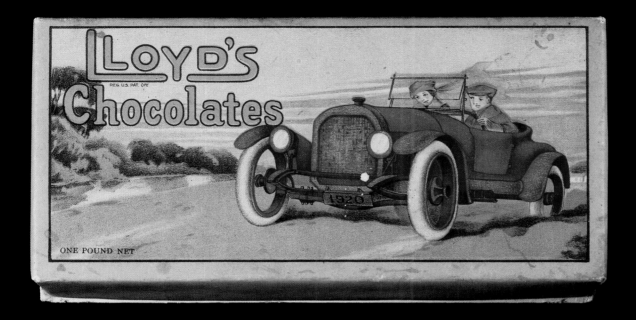

LLOYD'S
REG. U.S. PAT. OFF.
Chocolates

1920

ONE POUND NET

10¢ · 10¢
AUTO-LAKS
TRADE MARK
CHOCOLATES
A PLEASANT AND EASY PHYSIC.

ROWNTREE & YORK ENGLAND

STOP for Driver's CHOCOLATE CLUB

Clock

Marble, 8½ x 18⅜; France, ca. 1923. An Art Deco style motor clock made by Duplanid Clock Company of St. Etienne, France. Made of marble, the set includes two matching sconces with small medallions of St. Christopher holding the Christ child as protectors of those who travel.

TIMEPIECES

"The Mors Limousine"

Mixed media, 11⅞ x 17⅛; France, 1906. Oftentimes mistaken for a Renault limousine in catalogue descriptions, this high-quality French art object was given by the majarisha of Indore (Punjab) in India to "Diamond Jim Brady" when he visited San Francisco during a world tour in 1906. The object incorporates a functional eight hour clock, barometer and thermometer as insets in the compartment door panels, and had gilt and silver originally highlighting some of its features. Small rubies and diamonds were originally centered in the headlamps and sidelamps. The rear wheel can be wound, allowing all four wheels to rotate, giving the impression of forward motion. From the Thirties until his passing, the object was in the private collection of James Melton.

"The Motorist"

White metal, 15⅛ x 3⅝; Austria, ca. 1908. *(opposite)* The counterbalanced swing arm clock moves back-and-forth in the right arm of the figurine. The Swiss movement is by Tage.

"La Reine du Jour"

Emile Brouchon. Mixed media, 21¼ x 15½; France, ca. 1898. A very early automotive motif mantel clock with accompanying sconces artistically created by Emile Brouchon, who studied under the noted sculptor Mathurin Moreau. Brouchon first exhibited in Paris in 1880 and achieved prominence in statuary objects. Made of white metal, this classic Art Nouveau timepiece sits on an Italian marble base, contains a Swiss movement and is highlighted with a hand-painted ceramic clock face. The Goddess of Speed guiding the allegorical motor car was favored in artistic expression of early motor car races. The clock was manufactured by the Metris Clock Company of Rouen, France.

265

Commemorative Watches

These watches were given to drivers and mechanics and later to "pit crew" members by car manufacturers, motor clubs and motor product firms.

Top row, left to right:

The Tavannes Watch Company. The metal face cover depicts two occupants in the gondola of a Montgolfier-styled hot air balloon, while the reverse side details two men in a period racing car.

This nickel alloy watch features an angelic lady guiding the early motor car, the classic image of the early Gordon Bennett races.

Second row, left to right:

Of known French manufacture, this sterling silver watch depicts a driver and mechanic at speed in a city-to-city race with number 94 inscribed on the license plate.

An artist named Kogdebin designed the image on this case. Consisting of iodized metal, sterling silver and copper inlay, it depicts two cars racing in an urban setting, while the reverse side portrays a family on tour.

A sterling silver watch manufactured by Systeme Roskopf with a Spanish movement. The image depicts a Renault with occupants driving, while a cyclist passes the bridge above.

Bottom row, left to right: All of these watches were made of nickel or brass alloys in America before 1910.

A nickel alloy watch made by Ingersoll Company of Waterbury, Connecticut.

This watch was inspired by a car driven in the Vanderbilt Cup Race and was manufactured by the Elgin Watch Company.

The gold watch was made by an unknown New England manufacturer.

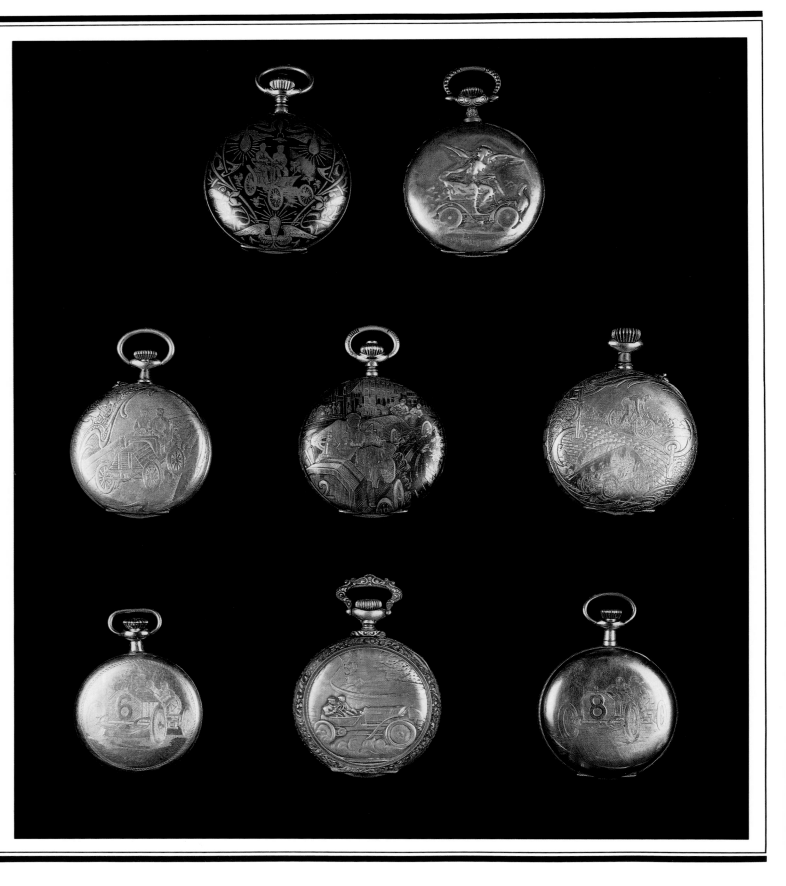

Touring Watches

Watches made wonderful gifts for friends, family or participants of early motoring days, with larger watches for men and smaller for women. These watches are touring watches.

Top row: Watches made of nickel alloy, produced by the Charriere Company in France, ca. 1906.

Second row: The watch on the left depicts a man and woman driving their early motor car in a setting of sunflowers and other fauna. Manufactured by Systeme Roskops, France, ca. 1907; the lady's watch was produced by Miracle Watch Company, France, ca. 1905.

Third row: The watch on the left was made by Oda, France, ca. 1905, and that on the right by A. Reymond Company of Zurick, Switzerland, ca. 1907. The movement is seven jewel, with parts of the case made in France.

Bottom row: Raised relief facets highlight the tourists of this turn-of-the-century watch made by Superior Timekeeper, while the sterling silver watch on the right was produced by the Congress Watch Company around 1905. Both were made in America.

Timing Watch

Nickel alloy, 3¼ d.; America, ca. 1904. This large watch has a two-seat open touring car on its face cover. Given as a "Special Award -St. Louis World Fair 1904," watches of this size were often used to record racing times with two or more persons monitoring the timepiece to assure greater accuracy.

Gold Watch

Eighteen-karat gold, 2½ x 1⅝; Swiss, ca. 1933. This attractive Art Deco watch in the shape of a European-designed radiator was made by the Mido Watch Company.

Cane Handle

Sterling silver, 2⅞ x 4⅜;
Germany, 1910. *(left)*

"Panhard & Levassor-
La Journee D'une Panhard"

Andre Nevil. Paper, 8 x 15½;
France. *(above)* Hand fan.

Pencil Holders

Mixed media, 3¼; ca. 1906-1910.
Pencil holders with auto images
in relief on the outside case
were used to record times and
fulfill diaries of motoring
events. The product was
promoted by Eberhard Faber,
the prominent pencil
manufacturer.

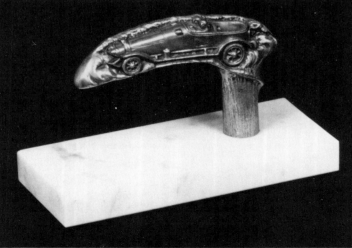

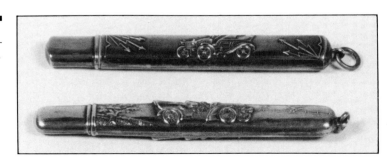

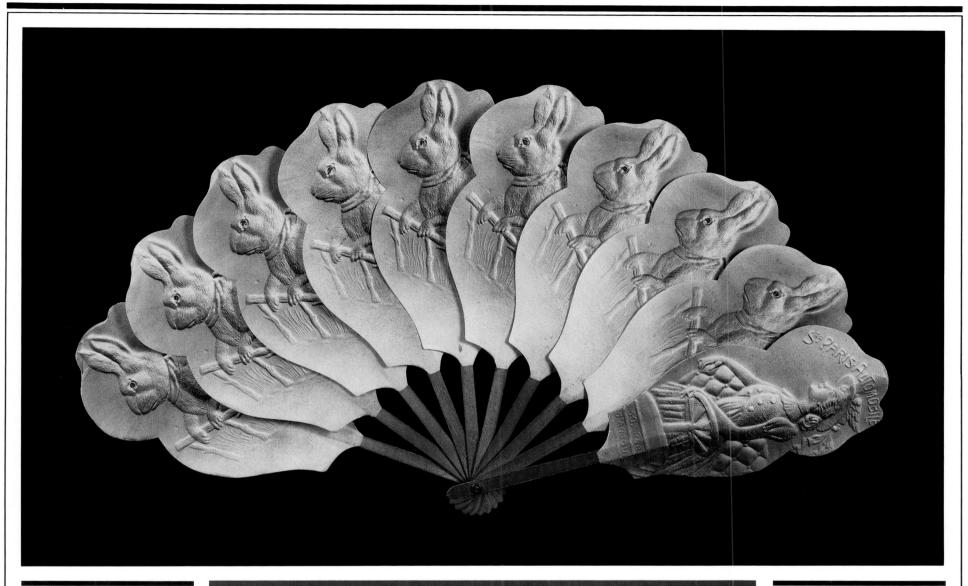

Hand Fan

Paper, 8 x 14¼; France, ca. 1907. Given as a token gift to members of the Automobile Society of Paris, this fan features the marques of Itala, Mercedes, Panhard-Levassor, Germaine, Napier and Mors.

Call Switch

Mixed media, 3⅞ x 1⅜; Germany, ca. 1910. A rare, hand-held call switch used to ring a servant's bell from the bedroom or table. Made of brass with electrical components and an ivory button.

Pipes

Sizes range 1½-2 x 5⅛-6½. Clockwise from top left:

Automotive meerschaum pipe with case. Ivory; Germany, 1901.

LeChauffer. Hand-carved. Ivory; French, 1905.

Touring car pipe, hand-carved hardwood. France, 1910.

Automotive pipe bowl. Ivory; Germany, ca. 1899.

Meerschaum pipe with male and female motorists. Ivory; ca. 1903.

Cigarette Cases

A variety of cases displayed in a converted Rolls-Royce radiator frame. *(opposite)*

Top row: open touring cars from 1910 through 1928.

Middle row, left to right: female motorists in a late nineteenth-century vehicle; two men escorting a female passenger, ca. 1899; and a couple driving in the country with their chauffeur in the rear seat.

Bottom row: Touring images common to the times. All cases in this row date from 1904 through 1914.

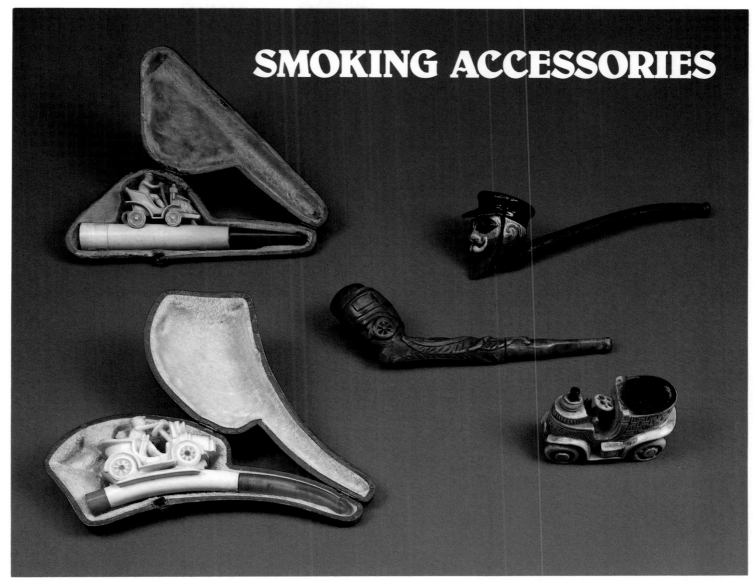

SMOKING ACCESSORIES

Cigarette Cutters

Nickel alloy, 1¾ x ⅝; Germany, ca. 1906. *(left)*

"Bebe Peugeot"

2¼ x 5; France, ca. 1901. *(right)* This pipe was given by company officials after the company first produced the one-cylinder Bebe Peugeot in 1901. Completely simple and reliable, the car gained tremendous popularity in the European marketplace.

Match Safes

Top row, left to right:

Lady's match safe. Sterling silver; England, ca. 1903.

Radiator-style match safe. Sterling silver and wood; England, ca. 1912.

Pratt's Motoring Products match safe. Sterling silver; England, ca. 1905.

Cigarette paper case. Alfred Schickerling Jewelry Company, Silver; America, 1910.

Middle row, left to right:

Bleriot Oxygen and Oil match safe. Brass; France, ca. 1910.

''Vices'' match safe. Alloy; ca. 1912. Features hand-painted ceramic inlays of woman, wine, gambling, and motoring.

Cigarette lighter. Brass, America, ca. 1910.

Bottom row, left to right:

''Fern-Croft Inn'' match safe. Nickel alloy; America, 1907. Sold to motorists visiting the inn. Made by M.W. Carr and Company, Massachusetts.

''My Motor Match'' match safe. Nickel alloy; England, ca. 1906.

Coney Island photographic image match safe. Brass alloy; America, 1903. Images show the entrances to Luna Park and Surf Drive.

Cigarette Cases

The following cigarette cases were awarded to personages involved with the motoring industry: drivers, mechanics, support personnel, manufacturers and so forth.

Top row, left to right:

This object was given to a personage with the initials "A.W.R." for the participation in a tourist race held on the "Bavarian Circuit" in 1922.

A case with Camille "Red Devil" Jenatzy driving his number 4 Mercedes. Jenatzy was the first person to achieve 100 km. per hour in 1899 in an electric, aluminum body vehicle called "La Jamais Contente." He later won the Gordon Bennett Race in Ireland, and had the artist Gaudy create the image found on this case. It was also used on advertising posters for Jenatzy's tire business.

After a grueling 15 hours, 33 minutes and six seconds, Fournier in his Mors arrived in Berlin to win the "Heavy Cars" division of the 1902 Paris-to-Berlin Race. This piece, which is believed to have been Fournier's personal case, commemorates the event.

Middle row, left to right:

Of unknown origin, this case depicts a rare image of a race car from a rear angle pose, ca. 1928.

While not a racing car, the image is a Daimler. The case was a gift in 1916 to Paul Daimler, son of Gottlieb Daimler. Daimler, like his father, made monumental contributions to the development of automotive technology, one example being the honeycombed radiator on the first Mercedes.

This case commemorates Gondoin in his Panhard, participating in the Paris-to-Berlin Race of 1902. Gondoin placed 32nd in the "Light Cars" division, averaging 27.1 mph.

Bottom, left to right:

Attributed to a participant with the initials "J.O.B." in the Royal Automobile Club's "Tourist Trophy" race held in 1908. The image is highlighted with blue and white enamel inlay.

Rich and colorful flora provides the background for this driver and mechanic coming at speed through a turn in a Gordon Bennett Race, ca. 1904.

An unknown driver and mechanic in a Gordon Bennett Race, ca. 1904.

Blue Bird Cases

Sterling silver; England, ca. 1930. Two different styles of cases used as advertising pieces for the Blue Bird Petrol Company. Left: 3¼ x 2⅝; right: 3 x 3¾.

Cigarette Cases

Mercedes-Benz. Metal, 1913-1922. These cases were gifts from the Benz Motorvagen Company to women smokers who purchased or assisted their husbands in the purchase of a car. This image is the most requested for reproduction from the Mercedes-Benz archives. The Benz Company changed the costume of the lady every several years, so the image provides a costume history of women in that period.

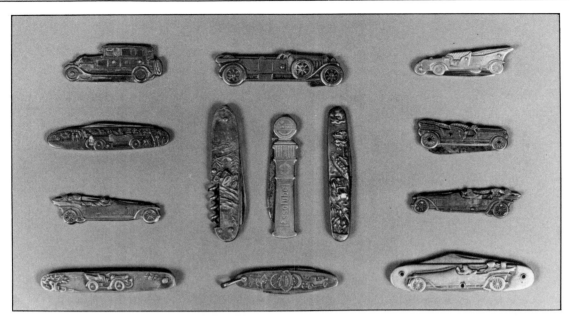

Pocketknives

A collection of common pocketknives that would accompany the motorist on tour, they were purchased as souvenirs, gifts or given by manufacturers to promote their products. All are made of mixed metals unless otherwise noted. Clockwise, from top left:

Solinger Company, Germany, 1922.

Coursolise, France, ca. 1912.

Designed by D. Peres, Solinger Cutlery, Germany, ca. 1910.

Germany, 1910.

Aratene Cutlery Company, Germany, ca. 1910.

America, ca. 1914.

Gift of ''L.C. Chaser Company, Boston, Massachusetts,'' manufactured by Robbin Company, America, ca. 1908.

Made by George Wostenholm, Sheffield, England, ca. 1911.

Aratene Cutlery, Germany, ca. 1913.

Wadsworth and Son, Germany, ca. 1909.

''Behold St. Christopher then go on your way to safety,'' Besset, England, 1912.

Gift premium of Esso Lube Standard Oil, manufactured by Dassau, France, ca. 1914.

England, ca. 1910.

Flasks

Glass and metal, 4½ to 6¾ x 2⅞ to 4½; England, ca. 1900. Before the motor car evolved into a closed compartment with substantial heating devices in the mid-Nineteen-thirties, maintaining body heat while driving was a serious, and occasionally life-threatening problem, particularly in a winter breakdown situation. Spirit flasks, filled with liquor or other alcohol derivatives supplied the driver and passengers through such times. As the car ''closed up'' so did the need for such decanters, thus increasing the technology of the automobile as well as its safety.

One-pint flask, Sterling silver, England, 1910.

Cylinder Oil ¾ pint flask. Silver and brown glass; England, ca. 1902.

One-pint flask engraved ''RP.'' Derby Silver, Ltd. England, ca. 1904.

Stamp Holder

Gilbert Wright. Glass and
sterling silver with lithograph,
1¹/₂ x 4¹/₈; England, ca. 1905.

Domestic Items

Sizes range 4 to 6 x 5¼ to 12¾.

Top: Lady's glove box. Cloth applied to cardboard, France, ca. 1903.

Lower left: Sewing set consisting of a dozen spools of various colored thread, needles, pins, celluloid sheath thimbles and a paper measuring tape. Distributed by the Haband Company of Paterson, New Jersey, the container and compartments were made in France with Haband providing the sewing materials for the package.

Lower right: Lady's jewelry box. Cloth applied to cardboard; France, ca. 1903.

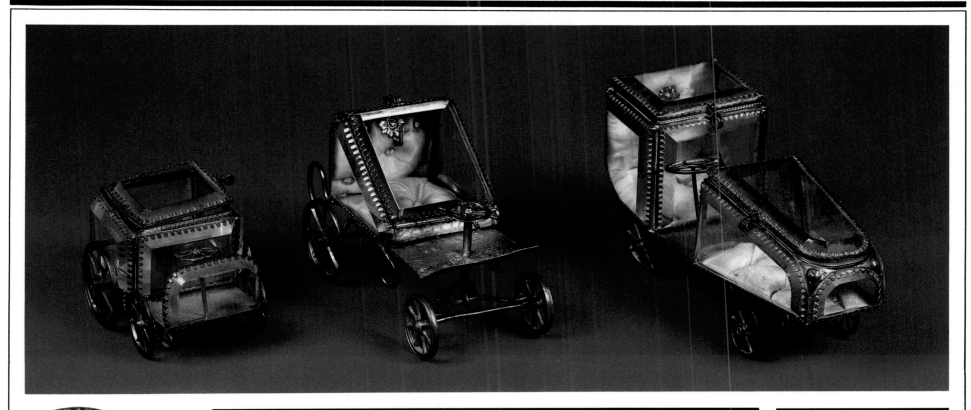

Jewelry Cases

Mixed Media, 3-4 x 4¼-7⅝; France, 1902-1910. Tin and brass metal pieces are used for the structure in these cars, while the crystal glass that forms the body is beveled. The jewelry compartment was lined with colored linens, some of which were padded.

Buttons

Brass and tin, 1⅝ x 2; France, ca. 1903. Delightful brass and tin coat buttons would highlight any men's driving coat of the period.

Styling Set

Mixed media, 8¾ x 4¼; France, ca. 1903. A coiffure styling set consisting of a brush and mirror glass with a lithograph image of a young female motorist. The handle is made of pressed tin highlighted by a voluptuous mermaid.

Women's Boxes

Left: "Paraphernalia Box." 4 x 12½; American, 1900. The box, containing manicure, buttonhook and sewing sets, is made of metal with ivory handles, while the automotive image on the lid is a lithograph pressed onto celluloid.

Right: Collar box. 4 x 9; America, ca. 1898. Originally used as a collar box, the interior base compartment was removed and used for some other storage purpose.

Mother of Pearl

Oyster shell, 3½ X 5⅞; America, ca. 1901. (above) Oyster shell "mother of pearl" objects originated in France and were highly popular in the American marketplace by 1900. Framed in tin, this lady's ink well and pin cushion adorned the desk around 1901.

Straight Razor

Mixed media, 6 h.; Germany, ca. 1910. These ivory handled straight razors were manufactured by the William Elliot Company of Germany for Shumate Cutlery Company of St. Louis, Missouri.

Decorations

Sizes range 1½-2½ x 1 ½-3½; A series of ceramic vessels hold hundreds of cuff links, brooches, medallions, buttons, hat pins, and other decorative adornments worn by the men and women motoring enthusiasts of the period.

Tabletop Cases

Sizes range $4^{1}/_{8}$-$8^{3}/_{8}$ x $7^{7}/_{8}$-$12^{5}/_{8}$. Clockwise, from left:

A Mercedes-inspired men's jewelry case is attributed to an unknown German manufacturer, ca. 1924.

A jewelry case of wood and beveled-glass windows, leather fenders and a music box. Germany, ca. 1924.

A jewelry case of wood with leather over tin fenders. Germany, ca. 1925.

A cigarette dispenser case with replaceable match strikers built into the running board. An ashtray slides from underneath the car when bumper is pulled. Inlaid wood; Germany, ca. 1903.

Boxes

Sizes range $3^{3}/_{4}$-$4^{1}/_{2}$ x $8^{5}/_{8}$-$12^{1}/_{2}$.

Top, left to right:

Spain, ca. 1905. A gentleman's jewelry case of wood with eight compartments and a bronze inlaid plaque of a racing car. The case was manufactured by Scovero of Madrid, Spain.

America, 1908. A lady's silver-plate glove box crafted by Wilcox Company of Meriden, Connecticut.

Bottom, left to right:

Cigarette/Cigar Case. Metal alloy with a bronze bas relief inlaid in the lid; France, ca. 1906.

Cigar case. Silver, America, ca. 1905. A cedar lined cigar case made of silver and oftentimes used in the United States as a commemorative gift for participation in the Vanderbilt Cup Races.

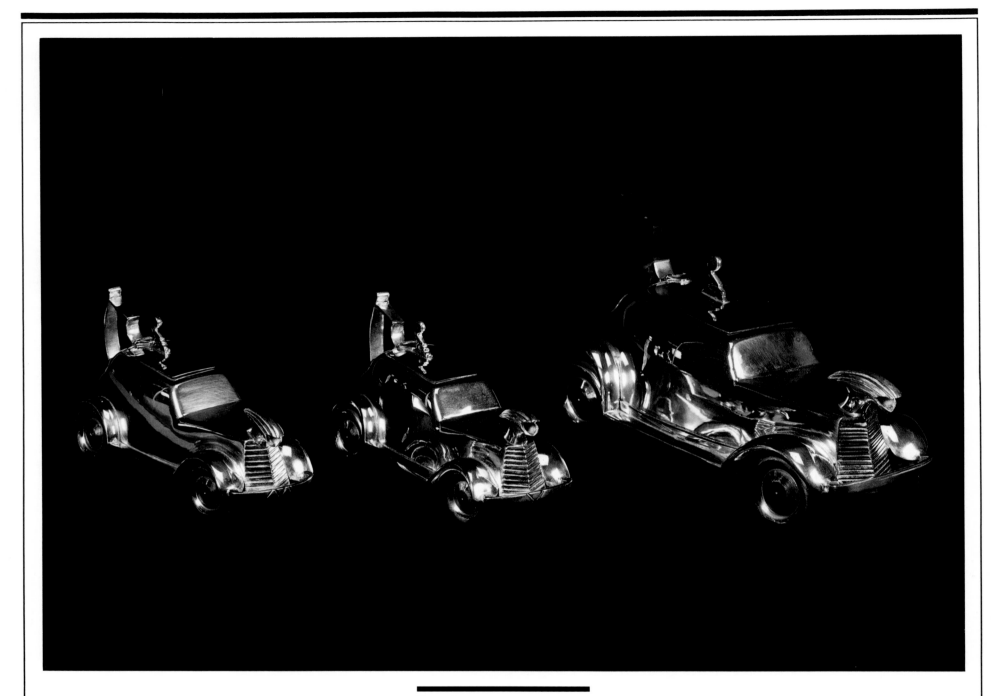

Tea pot

Sterling and celluloid, 4½ x
10¾ (pot) and 3⅜ x 7⅛
(creamers); France, 1922. A
fashionable tea pot with
creamers given as a gift by
Renault reflects the emerging
Art Deco designs of the early
Nineteen-twenties in the world
of art. The tea pots are made of
sterling with a celluloid handle.

Automotive Favors

Mixed media, 2 x 3; Germany, 1903–1914. Favors such as these would be inscribed with the guest's name, placed above the table setting and filled with candies or mints. These die-cut, heavy paper motor cars were highlighted with dried flowers and packaged six per box.

Toaster Rack

Sterling silver, 3¼ x 6; England, 1900. A hallmarked, Sheffield sterling silver toaster rack allowed enthusiasm for the motor car to be expressed at the breakfast table.

Napkin Ring Holders

Silver, 1½ x 1⅞; Germany, ca. 1911. *(above)*

Name Card Holders

Solinger. Silverplate, 1⅛ x 2⅝; Germany, ca. 1912. *(below)*

Card Holders

Both are of the same set. *(above)*

Left: Table card holder. Sterling silver, 1½ x 2½; England, ca. 1910.

Right: Table name card holder. Sterling silver, ¾ x 1³/₁₆; England, ca. 1910.

Name Card Holders

Solinger. Silver, 1¼ x 1⅝;
Germany, 1910. Used at dinner
parties to seat guests.

Cases

Wood, 2 to 2⅝ x 5 to 8;
England, ca. 1910. *(opposite)*

Top: Both items are cedar-lined cases made of metal alloy with sterling silver relief inlaid over mahogany for contrast.

Bottom: Both items utilize pecan wood in their manufacture.

Smoking Accessories

These English items are made of nickel alloy and incorporated lithograph art work of Gilbert Wright, the noted English equestrian artist of the late Eighteen-nineties who painted motoring scenes after 1900.

Top: Desk Tray.

Middle row, left to right: Matchbox, Cigarette/cigar box, cigarette case.

Bottom: Glass ashtray.

Container

Celluloid, 4 x 7¾; France, ca. 1925. *(left)* This object was used to hold jewelry or cigarettes and matches, depending on the design of the interior compartment inserts.

Cigar and Cigarette Case

Gilbert Wright. Sterling silver, 2¼ x 6⅞; England, ca. 1900. *(right)* Two Gilbert Wright scenes highlight this sterling silver, cedar-lined cigar and cigarette case presented to ''Reginald L. Reeves by the Gentlemen of the Holy Trinity Choir, Maidstone, Easter 1906.''

Desk Set

Brass, 2⅞-7¼ x 2-7¼; England, 1905. *(above)* An automotive desk set consisting of a thermometer, perpetual calendar, expandable bookrack and letter-holder.

Desk Caddy

William Furick. Silver, 6⅜ x 15⅜; Germany, ca. 1910. One of a series of desk pieces created by William Furick, this one is based upon a Mercedes. Furick's automotive-subject work was also completed in pewter and bronze. Such pieces were given out by automobile clubs to drivers placing well in events.

Picture Frames

Automotive image photo frames were popular before World War I, and given as prizes on tours as well as gifts by motor car and insurance companies. These frames were produced from 1900 through 1914 and captured some of the scenes and events of early motoring times. Sizes range from 1¾ x 3¼ to 2 x 3½.

Top row, left to right:

Sterling silver with rhinestones; France, ca. 1904.

Brass; English, ca. 1905.

''K.S.'' Sterling silver; England, ca. 1904.

Brass with lithograph touring scene; England, ca. 1903.

Middle row, left to right:

An Art Nouveau styled frame made of silver and produced by Solinger of Germany, ca. 1904.

Tin and cast iron; America, ca. 1914.

Solinger. Silver; Germany, ca. 1905.

Bottom row, left to right:

Brass photo frame pin made of silver plate, copper and bronze promoting Flint, Michigan as ''Vehicle City'' in 1908.

Signed by an artisan with the initial ''B,'' this souvenir favor has a small hand-painted automotive image in its viewing compartment. England, ca. 1905.

Opium Box

Laminated wood, 1½ x 9; ca. 1914. This item features six decoupage images, one of a motoring scene, reflecting the activities of the Shakespeare Company. The lettering on the case is Arabic.

Photo Album

Mixed materials, 10⅞ x 14⅞;
France, ca. 1909. Embossed
cover featuring five modes of
human transportation highlights
this 74-page album.

Trays

Sizes range $5^3/8$ to $6^1/2$ x $6^3/8$ to $9^7/8$.

Top left: A silver-plate tray, Germany, ca. 1900.

Top right: A Mercedes-inspired card tray. Silver plated, Germany, ca. 1903.

Bottom: A silver card-tray, probably given to participants in a city-to-city race, Germany, ca. 1902.

Photo Album

Cardboard, 3 x $8^3/4$; America, ca. 1900. Photo albums were often presented to couples who participated in automotive touring events, even though they could be purchased outright from catalogue sources. Such albums were made of cardboard with lithograph images on celluloid covers. Motorists placed photos (which were rare) of their tour in the album and in some cases, plant specimens gleaned from along the tour were also pressed and saved. This album held a maximum of 53 photographs and contains work by photographers such as Paul Linert of Dresden, Germany and David Scannell and George Samon of Philadelphia, Pennsylvania.

Ashtrays

Automotive ashtrays have been popular as souvenirs since the earliest days of motoring. Clockwise from top left:

Bronze; England, ca. 1905.

Brass; England, ca. 1905.

Bronze; France, 1907.

Tin alloy; France, 1908. Ashtray by "J.S. and S. B." and stamped for giveaways at Daimler's showrooms in Coventry, Nottingham, Bristol and London.

Automotive Ashtrays

Right: Metal alloy, Germany, ca. 1925.

Far right: "Automobile Club of France" logo stamped in metal by Medaille D'Or of Paris, ca. 1899. The Art Nouveau relief image was created by J. Callo and is similar in style to earlier works by Daniel Dupuis.

Matchbox Holder

Brass, 9⅝ x 5; England, ca. 1915. A wall-mounted matchbox holder.

Letter Openers

Most letter openers were "hand-out" gifts to customers purchasing a motorcar or an automotive related supply or service. Top to bottom:

Designed and produced by Cartier, with global distribution offices in New York, Paris and London, this mid-Thirties object was made out of sterling silver. It depicts a racing scene with five cars. For the convenience of the right-handed user, the opener's handle is a powerful magnifying lens. The piece was magnificently packaged and sold in the lined burgundy box with brass clasps.

The Greenduck Company produced this letter opener for the Lord Motor Car Company of Los Angeles, California. The image is an aerial view of a seven-passenger Studebaker. Nickel alloy, 1919.

Produced by the Magnetic Cutlery Company of Philadelphia in the mid-Teens, this item was exported to D. Peres and Affiliates, of Solingen, Germany. The handle depicts an open touring car.

An open touring car over the word "Protection" is the prominent feature of this gift given by the Insurance Company of the State of Pennsylvania. Brass, ca. 1920.

A Kelly Springfield Tire Company letter opener with the handle adorned with the image of a lady in the center of a production tire. Produced by Bastian Brothers Company of Rochester, this item was given throughout Kelly's distribution outlets in New York. Brass, 1916.

Made of brass, this object presents a mustachioed gentleman driving a race car. Origin is unknown, ca. 1906.

A unique, left-handed letter opener given by the Parisian Panhard et Lavassor Company via its New York offices at Broadway and 62nd St., NW corner. Brass, ca. 1910.

This large opener depicts the driver in an aerodynamically designed car, possibly a Bugatti showroom vehicle. Created by an obscure artist named Duval, the object is an outstanding example of the use of the automobile in the Art Deco period. Bronze, ca. 1934.

Bottom right, vertical: A lady's Scimitar letter opener depicts a woman at the wheel of an automobile on its handle. Believed to be of French production, the piece was made of a white metal alloy, ca. 1912.

Buckboard

Copper, 16 x 25; America, ca.
1898. Made in New England.

Gold Weathervane

Copper with gold paint, 13 x 28;
America, ca. 1907. Attributed to
Snow.

Boston Weathervane

Tin, 14 x 34¼; America, 1907.
Manufactured by the W.P.A.
Snow Iron Works Co., of 19
Portland St., Boston,
Massachusetts.

"Locomobile"

Paint over copper, 27 x 38;
America, 1910.

"Locomobile"

Copper, 24 x 41½; America,
1912. This weathervane was
available from about 1907 to
1914 from the E.G. Washburne
Co. in New York City.

BIBLIOGRAPHY

PAINT & INK

Abdy, Jane. *The French Poster.* New York: Clarkson N. Potter, Inc., 1985.

Automobile Club of France. *Le Salon de L'Affiche Automobile.* Paris, 1978.

Banister, Manley. *Etching & Other Intaglio Techniques.* New Jersey: Littlefield, Adams & Co., Totawa, 1974.

The Beauty of Cars, Introduction by Kenneth Ullyett. New York: Pitman Publishing Corp.

Caricature: The Wit and Humor of a Nation in Picture, Song, & Story. New York: Leslie-Judge Co.

Chene. *J.H. Lartigue et les Autos.* Paris: 1974.

Clay, Jean. *Modern Art 1890-1918.* New York: The Vendome Press, 1978.

Clymer, Floyd. *Indianapolis Race History Complete Detailed History of Every Indianapolis Race since 1909.* Los Angeles: 1946.

Clymer, Floyd. *Treasury of Early American Automobiles 1877-1925.* New York: McGraw-Hill Book Co., Inc., 1950.

Demand, Carlo. *Motor Racing Sketchbook.* London: G.T. Foulis & Co., Ltd.

Fielding, Mantle. *American Painters, Sculptors and Engravers.* Poughkeepsie: Apollo Book, 1984.

Flagg, James Montgomery and Susan E. Meyer. New York: Watson-Guptill Publications, Div. of Billboard Publications, Inc., 1974.

Frostick, Michael. *Advertisement & The Motor-Car.* London: Lund Humphries Publishers, Ltd., 1970.

Gifford, Pierre. *La Fin du Cheval.* Paris: Armand Colin & Cir, 1899.

Master of the Poster 1896-1900. New York: Images Graphiques, Inc., 1977.

Mathieson, T.A.S.O. *Grand Prix Racing 1906-1914.* 1965.

Miscellaneous Man Catalog 23. New Freedom: Rare Vintage Posters, 1986.

''Motoring Milestones'' 10th in a series of portfolios from the pages of *Autocar.* London: I.P.C. Transport Press, Ltd., 1979.

O'Galop. *L'Auto K.6.0.20.* Paris: Gainier Freres, 1905.

The Pierce-Arrow Motor Car Co., Buffalo & Erie County Historical Society, Vol. XXV, #3, 1978.

Pitz, Henry C. *200 Years of American Illustration.* New York: Random House, Inc., 1977.

Reed, Walt, and Roger Reed. *The Illustrator in America 1880-1980.* New York: Madison Square Press, Inc., 1984.

Rennert, Jack. *Prize Posters.* New York: Poster Auctions International, Inc., 1985.

Silk, Gerald. *Auto and Culture.* New York: Harry N. Abrams, Inc., 1984.

Society of Illustrators. *The Society of Illustrators 26th Annual of American Illustrators.* New York: Madison Square Press Inc., 1985.

Weill, Alain. *The Poster.* Massachusetts: G. K. Hall & Co., 1985

Zeller, Von Reimar. *Automobil.* Germany: Insel Verlag, 1985.

Zeppegno, C. *Cara Automibile,* Torino: Industrie Grafiche, 1968.

METALWORK

Beaulieu, Lord Montagu of, and F. Wilson McComb. *Behind the Wheel.* New York: Paddington Press, Ltd., 1977.

Celant, Germano. *Auto Tattoo.* Bruno Alfieri-Publisher.

Copper Weathervanes Manufactured by J. W. Fiske-1893. Des Moines: Wallace-Homestead Book Co., The Pyne Press, 1971.

Davis, S.C.H. *Mercedes-Benz.* London: Frederick Muller Ltd., 1956.

Dejean, Philippe. *Bugatti.* New York: Rizzoli International Publications, Inc., 1982.

Eaglesfield, Barry. *The Bugatti Book.* London: Motor Racing Publications, Ltd., 1954.

Important, Early & Classic Motor Vehicles, Automobile Art. London: Sotheby, March, 1989.

Kimes, Beverly Rae. *The Star and the Laurel.* Montvale: Mercedes-Benz of North America, Inc., 1986.

Knight, J. K. *Notes on Motor Carriages.* London: Hazell, Watson & Viney, Ltd., 1896.

Mathieson, T.A.S.O. *Historic du Grand Prix de l'ACF 1906-1914.* 1965.

Pomeroy, Lawrence. *The Grand Prix Car 1906-1939.* Berks: Motor Racing Publicatons Ltd., 1949.

Prinz Heinrich-Fahrt und bilder aus dem Sportleben, Continental- Caouchouc und Gutta - Percha-Campagnie, Hanover.

Robson, Graham. *Mercedes.* New York: W. H. Smith Publishers, Inc., 1988.

Schuster, George with Tom Mahoney. *The Longest Auto Race.* New York: John Day Co., Inc., 1962.

The Vintage Racing Machine, Cars from the Collection of George H. Waterman, Jr., Museum of Art, Rhode Island School of Design,1970.

Williams, William C. *Motoring Mascots of the World.* Osceola: Motorbooks International Publishers & Wholesales, Inc.

CERAMICS

Atterbury, Paul. *The History of Porcelain.* New York: William Morrow & Co., Inc., 1982.

Davis, S. C. H. *Casque's Sketch Book.* London: Iliffe and Sons Limited.

Dodd, A. E. *Dictionary of Ceramics.* New Jersey: Littlefield, Adams & Co., Inc., 1967.

Hillier, Bevis. *The World of Art Deco.* (An exhibition organized by the MN Institute of Arts). New York: E. P. Dutton, 1971.

Huxford, Sharon and Bob. *Roseville Pottery.* Kentucky: Collector Books, 1980.

Ketchum Jr., William C. *Pottery & Porcelain, The Knopf Collectors' Guide to American Antiques.* New York: Alfred A. Knopf, Inc., 1983.

Man and the Motor Car. New Jersey Div. of Motor Vehicles, 1949.

Motor Clothing, Birmingham: The Dunlop Rubber Co., Ltd.

Nelson, Glenn C. *Ceramics: A Potter's Handbook.* New York: Susan Katz, 1984.

Stitt, Irene. *Japanese Ceramics of the Last 100 Years.* New York: Crown Publishers, Inc., 1974.

MIXED MEDIA

Dorsey, Hebe. *Age of Opulence: The Belle Epoque in the Paris Herald 1890-1914.* New York: Harry N. Abrams, Inc., 1987.

Lambourne, Lionel. *Utopian Craftsmen.* (Astragal Books) London: The Architectural Press, Ltd., 1980.

Sears, Stephen W. *The Automobile in America.* New York: American Heritage Publishing Co., Inc., 1977.

Wilson, Richard Guy, Dianne H. Pilgrim, and Dickran Tashjian. *The Machine Age in America 1918-1941.* New York: Harry N. Abrams, Inc., 1986.

PLAYTHINGS

American Children's Vehicles. Catalog of the American National Co., Ohio.

Barenholtz, Bernard, and Inex McClintock. *American Antique Toys 1830-1900.* NY: Harry N. Abrams, Inc., 1980.

Cieslik, Jurgen and Marianne. ''Pageant of Toys.'' *The History of E. P. Lehman - 1881-1981.* New Cavendish Books, 1982.

Culff, Robert. *The World of Toys.* Middlesex: The Hamlyn Publishing Group, Ltd., 1969.

Fraser, Antonia. *A History of Toys*. Delacorte Press.

Gardiner, Gordon and Alistair Morris. *The Price Guide to Metal Toys*. Suffolk: Antique Collector's Club, 1980.

Gardiner, Gordon, and Alistair Morris. *The Illustrated Encyclopedia of Metal Toys*. New York: Harmony Books, Div. of Crown Publishers, Inc., 1984.

Gottschalk, Lillian. *American Toy Cars & Trains & Trucks 1894-1942*. New York: Abbeville Press, 1985.

Gottschalk, Lillian. *American Toy Cars & Trucks*. New York: Abbeville Press, Inc., 1985.

Jouets Automobiles 1890-1939. La Collection Peter Ottenheimer. London: Denys Ingram Publishers, 1894.

King, Constance Eileen. *The Encyclopedia*. New York: Crown Publishers, Inc., 1978.

King, Constance E. *Toys & Dolls*. New York: Rizzoli International Publications, Inc., 1979.

Moran, Brian. ''Battery Toys.'' *The Modern Automata*. PA: Schiffer Publishing, Ltd., 1984.

Pressland, David. *The Art of the Tin Toy*. Great Britain: New Cavendish Books, 1976.

Remise, Jac, and Jean Fondin. *The Golden Age of Toys*.

Schiffer, Margaret. *Christmas Ornaments*. Pennsylvania: Schiffer Publishing Ltd., 1984.

Schraeder, Jr., Joseph J. *The Wonderful World of Toys, Games & Dolls*. Illinois: DBI Books, Inc.

Schwartz, Marvin. *F.A.O. Schwartz Toys Through the Years*. New York: Doubleday & Co., Inc., 1975.

Toys, Dolls, Militaria Collectibles. Auction Catalog Massachusetts: Robert Skinner Inc., 1984.

Whitton, Blair. *A History of Toys 1862-1900*. Pennsylvania: Schiffer Publishing, 1981.

DAILY LIFE

Bergevin, Al. *Tobacco Tins and Their Prices*. Illinois: Wallace-Homestead Book Co., 1986.

Clymer, Floyd. *Indianapolis Race History 1946 Supplement*. California.

Complete Handbook of Automobile Hobbies. New Jersey: Automobile Quarterly, Princeton Publishing, Inc., 1981.

Fox, Jack C. *The Illustrated History of the Indianapolis 500*. Indiana: Carl Hungness & Associates, 1975.

Karslake, Kent, and Lawrence Pomeroy. *From Veteran to Vintage: A History of Motoring & Motorcars from 1884-1914*. London: Temple Press, Ltd., 1956.

Klein, Dan, and Margaret Bishop. *Decorative Art 1880-1980*. London: Phaidon Christie's Ltd., 1986.

La Pendule Francaise dans le Monde, Volumes 1, 2, & 3. Paris: Tardy, 1987.

Mortimer, Charles. *The Constant Search*. England: Haynes Publications Group, March 1982.

Sotheby's Early and Classic Motor Vehicles, Automobilia and Automobile Art. London: 1989.

Stern, Philip Van Doren. *A Pictorial History of the Automobile*. New York: Viking Press, 1953.

Whitton, Blair. *The Knopf Collectors' Guides to American Antiques*. New York: Alfred A. Knopf, Inc., 1984.

Worthington-Williams, Michael. *Automobilia*. London: BT Botsford and the RAC.

GENERAL BIBLIOGRAPHY

American Heritage. American Heritage Publishing, Inc., Volume XIII, Number 3, 1962.

Andrews, Allen. *The Mad Motorists the Great Peking-Paris Race of '07*. Philadelphia: J. B. Lippincott Co., 1965.

Automobile Quarterly. Twenty Year Cumulative Index, Vol. 5, No. 2; Vol. 6, No 2; Vol. 11, No. 2; Vol. 11 No. 4; Vol. 12, No. 1; Vol. 12, No. 3; Vol. 15, No. 3; Vol. 22, No. 3; Vol. 26, No. 1. Kutztown, Pennsylvania: Automobile Quarterly Publications.

Banister, Manly. *Lithographic Prints from Stone & Plate*. New Jersey: Littlefield, Adams & Co., 1974.

Boddy, William. *The History of Motor Racing*. New York: G. P. Putnam's Sons, 1977.

Chicago History. The Magazine of the Chicago Historical Society, Fall and Winter, 1982.

Chronicle of the 20th Century. Mount Kisco: Chronicle Publications Inc., 1987.

Dumont, Pierre, Ronald Barker, and Douglas B. Tubbs. *Automobiles & Automobiling 1900-1940*. Bonanza Books.

Duncan. H. O. *The World on Wheels*. Vol. 1. Paris: H. O. Duncan-Publisher.

Edge, S. F. *My Motoring Reminiscences*. England: G.T. Faulis & Co., Ltd.

The Evolution of the Motor Car in Pictures. Shrewsbury: The Museum of Transportation, 1933.

Fabre, Maurice. *A History of Land Transportation*. New York: Hawthorn Books, Inc., 1963.

Grun, Bernard. *The Timetables of History*. New York: Simon & Schuster, Inc., 1975.

Harter, Jim. *Transportation*. New York: Dover Publications, Inc., 1984.

Helck, Peter. *The Checkered Flag*. New York: Charles Scribner's Sons, 1961.

Helck, Peter. *Great Auto Races*. New York: Harry N. Abrams, 1975.

Hertz, Louis H. *Antique Collecting for Men*. New York: Hawthorn Books, Inc., 1969.

Hill, Mike. *Weird and Wonderful Autos*. New Jersey: Enterprise Books, 1975.

Hooper, W. Eden. *The Motor Car in the First Decade of the 20th Century.* London: Butterworth & Co., 1908.

Hornung, Clarence P. *Portrait Gallery of Early Automobiles*. New York: Harry N. Abrams, Inc.

Huber, Rudger. *Autos-Motorrader*. Munchen Fabreproduktionen: Battenberg Verlag, 1982.

Inomoto, Yoshihiro. *Automobile Illustration*. Tokyo: Nigensha Co., Ltd.

Jarrott, Charles. *Ten Years of Motors and Motor Racing*. England: Grant Richards Ltd., 1906.

Jones, Lois Swan. *Art Research*. 2nd ed. Dubuque: Kendall/Hunt Publishing Co., 1978.

Mayer, Ralph. *A Dictionary of Art Terms & Techniques*. New York: Thomas Y. Crowell Co., 1969.

Milleis International Antiques Price Guide. New York: Viking Penquin Inc., 1985.

Montagu, Lord. *The Gordon Bennett Races*. Cassell & Co., Ltd., 1965.

Nicholson, T. R. *The World's Motor Museums*. Philadelphia: J. B. Lippincott Co., 1970.

Phillips Sale Catalogues. London: Sale Numbers: 23,307, 23,201, 22,518, 22,899, 22,760,23,014, 509.

Pomeroy, Lawrence, *The Grand Prix Car 1906-1939*. England: Motor Racing Publications, Ltd., 1949.

Rand McNally Family World Atlas. Rand McNally & CO., 1985.

Rose, Barbara, *American Art Since 1900*. New York: Praeger Publishers, Inc., 1975.

Rose, Gerald. *A Record of Motor Racing*. London: The Royal Automobile Club, 1909.

Scientific American Publications. New York: Munn & Co., Feb. 1880, July 1895, Aug. 1895, Sept. 1895, Oct. 1895, Nov. 1895, Dec. 1895, Nov. 1897, June 1903.

Sears, Stephen W. *The Automobile in America*. New York: American Heritage Publishing Co., Inc., 1977.

Stein, Ralph. *The Great Inventions*. Chicago: Playboy Press, 1976.

Transport Pioneers of the Twentieth Century. Cambridge, England: Transport Trust, Ltd., 1981.

Tubbs, D.B. *Art and the Automobile*. England: Lutterworth Press, 1978.

The Winton Six 33. Ohio: The Winton Company, Cleveland, 1916.

INDEX TO THE ARTISTS